Pavel Demidov

**The jewish question in Russia**

Pavel Demidov

**The jewish question in Russia**

ISBN/EAN: 9783337102951

Printed in Europe, USA, Canada, Australia, Japan

Cover: Foto ©Lupo / pixelio.de

More available books at **www.hansebooks.com**

# THE JEWISH QUESTION

# IN RUSSIA.

BY

PRINCE DEMIDOFF SAN-DONATO.

*Translated from the Russian with the Author's permission*

By J. MICHELL,

H.M. CONSUL, ST. PETERSBURGH.

LONDON
DARLING AND SON,
MINERVA STEAM PRINTING OFFICE, 35, EASTCHEAP, E.C.

1884.

# CONTENTS.

|  | PAGE. |
|---|---|
| PREFACE - | v, vi. |
| INTRODUCTION - | vii–x |
| I. Historical Past of the Jews - | 1–9 |
| II. Brief Historical Sketch of Russian Legislation respecting the Jews - | 10–51 |
| III. Laws in force relating to the Jews - | 52–75 |
| IV. Density of Jewish Population and Economic Condition of Jews within the Limits of their Legal Domicile - - | 76–91 |
| CONCLUSION - - - - - - | 92–105 |
| APPENDICES - | 107–110 |

# PREFACE.

I AM personally indebted to Mr. J. MICHELL, Her Majesty's Consul at St. Petersburg, for his able translation of PRINCE DEMIDOFF's Pamphlet, "The Jewish Question in Russia," from the Russian language into English, having previously obtained his gracious permission, and also the special sanction of the English Foreign Office to undertake the work.

PRINCE DEMIDOFF DONATO's brochure merits the fullest consideration, seeing that the Author is one of the wealthiest members of the Russian Aristocracy, and is at the same time one of the largest employers of labour in that Empire. He is a man of known impartiality, and a great authority on the Jewish question, having studied it for thirteen years at Kiew. His arguments are clear and conclusive. The statistical and historical data collected by the Prince are extremely valuable, both from the point of view of the actual political question and the history of our

Russian co-religionists. It is really remarkable how little is known of the history of the largest community of Jews in the world. I consider I am rendering an eminent service to the English Jews in furnishing them, at my own cost, with this excellent study, but nothing to be compared to that rendered to the Jews of the whole world by the Prince, and for which they ought to be truly grateful.

H. GUEDALLA.

*April*, 1884.

# INTRODUCTION.

The main features of the Jewish question in Russia have already been treated by us in a short Memorandum,[1] and the present work presents only a development of the propositions therein laid down.

Without attempting to deal exhaustively with this important subject, our present object is to present the chief outlines of the position of Jews in Russia, as viewed from its economical bearings to the State.

In our opinion the essence of the Jewish question is in the abnormal social-economical condition of the life of the Russian Jews and Russian peasantry, which affords a convenient soil for the development of a spoliatory system of exploiting the resources and

---

[1] "A few words on the Jewish question, 1883."

productive powers of a country—a system which constitutes a crying evil in the present economical structure of the Russian labouring classes.

In most of the States of Western Europe where this evil also exists, and even perhaps in a higher degree than in Russia, the special modes of Jewish exploitation are altogether unknown, nor can it be said that any Jewish question exists.[1] There was, however, a time when those countries were also afflicted with such a question, and in a form similar to that now prevailing in Russia; this was namely the case when the Jews were a distinct class, deprived of the civil rights which were accorded to the native race, being thus ostracized as aliens and outcasts. But since the common rights of mankind have been extended to the Jews, and in countries where they have been placed on an equal footing as regards *civil status* with the citizens of other religious creeds, neither Jewish exclusiveness, nor systematic Jewish exploitation is visible; and yet it is chiefly to Western Europe that the Jews owe all the singularities of their

---

[1] The anti-semitic agitation of recent origin, which has manifested itself in some parts of Austria-Hungary and Germany is to be attributed in the first country to the prevalence of national discord, and in the second, to strife of political parties.

national characteristics, acquired by them during the long period of persecution to which they were exposed in the middle ages. The character, habits and pursuits of a people and their national idiosyncracies, generally formed under the influence of certain historical conditions, though transmissable from generation to generation, may yet gradually change and eventually disappear under the influence of new conditions of life, so soon as they no longer find a congenial soil for their culture and development. The exclusiveness and alienation of a certain portion of a population, or of an entire race, are generally the results of persecution under which individuals struggling to escape from the disadvantages of their position, closely ally themselves with those similarly situated. This phenomenon finds apt illustration in the history of the Jewish race, which commencing from its original "dispersion" to the end of the eighteenth century, was exposed to the most cruel oppression and restraint in its religious and economic life. The extreme ignorance, religious fanaticism, as well as national and social narrowmindedness of the period were the chief causes of the hostile attitude of the Christian populations towards the Jews. These factors manifest themselves throughout the whole history of the persecutions of the middle ages in Western Europe. But with the development of true civilization and humane principles, intolerance of, and enmity towards the Jews gradually grow less and less and finally disappear altogether to the tranquillity and well-being of the countries in which the Jews are domiciled.

# CHAPTER I.

SKETCH OF THE HISTORICAL PAST OF THE JEWS.

Having passed from a patriarchal form of tribal existence through that of an agricultural theocracy and of an Eastern Empire, the present Jewish people resolved themselves principally into an industrial and a trading community. This social formation proceeded from the "dispersion" of the race, which process commenced long before the Christian era and its final period may be reckoned from the time of the Romans to the epoch of persecutions in the middle ages. The constant apprehension of danger to their lives and property under which the Jews laboured was one of the main actuating causes of their preference of movable property to land. This predilection produced a whole series of generations severed from the soil and estranged from the plough; thus was a race produced incapable of bearing the strain of the constant and severe physical exertion which falls to the lot of the agriculturist.[1]

The history of the Jews in Western Europe divides itself into three periods, each differing in the spirit of the relations of the Christian population towards the

[1] M. Solovieff—Legends and traditions of the Talmud Vestnik Evropy for May, 1883, p. 149.

Jewish race; the first terminates with the commencement of the Crusades; the second lasts through these Crusades, while the third prevails from the end of the last century. Prior to the epoch of the Crusades the relations of Christians to the Jews were marked by a spirit of greater tolerance than that which was apparent during the succeeding period. Strong as religious fanaticism was even at that time, it was not then able to manifest itself in the form of such great cruelties as were practised against the heterodox Jews during the Crusades. Notwithstanding the animosity of the Christians towards the Jewish religion, the Jews were tolerated, and enjoyed considerable rights and general esteem as the depositaries and exponents of ancient classic lore, and particularly as the principal intermediaries in trade, in which the Christians, enthralled by their feudal agricultural organization, did not engage. The Jews, not being admitted into this organization, almost exclusively devoted their energies to trade, which was the only occupation indisputably left to them. At the same time, being scattered all over the world, they were easily able to establish international commercial relations with different countries, which considerably enlarged the sphere of their activity. But from the time of the Crusades the position of the Jews was entirely changed. Religious fanaticism took the sanguinary form which led to the complete brutalization of the masses. Hatred towards the Jews, as unbelievers, was excited and grew to such proportions that they were destroyed in great numbers by fire and sword. Even long after the wars of the Crusades hatred towards the Jews did not cease; the smallest spark was sufficient to kindle a conflagration which led to wholesale extermination of the Jewish population; with this object the most absurd accusations were made against the Jews, such as the use by them of Christian blood; desecration of the host; poisoning of wells; they were also accused of being the cause of all kinds of national calamities which visited this or that country, for instance as the plague; Siberian pestilence; black death, etc.[1]

After the Crusades the intolerance evinced towards the Jews in social economical respects grew in intensity. From this period trade and industry began to develope themselves among the Christian populations, who now strove to establish international commercial relations of their own and to drive the Jews from this sphere of human activity. In their struggle with feudalism the burgher classes formed themselves into

[1] Thus, in Franconia, in the town of Rettlingen, a certain Rindfleisch taking advantage of a false report respecting the pollution of the Host by a Jew proclaimed that he was "chosen by the Almighty to exterminate the Jews," and his instigations led to cruel persecutions. On the 20th April, 1298, the inflamed populace burned all the Jews in the town of Rettlingen, and then proceeded to massacre them in other towns and hamlets; in this manner, on the 24th July all the Jews in the town of Würzburg were killed; on the 1st August, those in Nürenburg met the same fate, and similar massacres subsequently took place in Mergenheim, Newmarket, Rotenburg, Bamberg, Aschberg, Parhing, Wildenstein, etc. From Franconia and Bavaria the movement spread to Austria, and in the course of six months 140 Jewish communities became the victims of fire and the sword. More than 100,000 Jews were slaughtered at this time.

The whole history of the middle ages, from the time of the Crusades, abounds with similar horrible events.

special corporations, commercial guilds and artisan associations, the special object all of which was to monopolise trade and handicrafts. Neither into guilds nor artificers' unions were the Jews received; while agriculture they were not able to pursue as a calling. In this manner only one occupation was left to them, that of usury, which in those days was the only form of credit that existed, and which could not be dispensed with. It must be observed, moreover, that the Jews all the more readily adopted this occupation, seeing that it could not be monopolised by the Christians, who by canonical law were strictly forbidden to lend out money at interest, while at the same time the Jews in many places were even *obliged* to advance money on pledges to all who applied to them. In this manner, both by custom and law the Jews were forced to become money-lenders, and they in this shape seemingly found compensation for being debarred from other pursuits. Lastly, frequently expelled and driven from country to country and treated as being beyond the pale of the law, the Jews found that money served them as the only means of salvation and enabled them to purchase their right to existence. Moreover, during this period of frequent expulsions, money could be more readily concealed than any other kind of movable property. Thus, dating from the Crusades, to religious oppression was added a persecution of the Jews in pecuniary respects, which, while impelling them on the path of unproductive pursuits, increased at the same time the general animosity against them. It is only at this period that historical records begin to contain complaints about the Jews despoiling the people. In Germany, especially, the Jews were exposed to the bitterest persecutions, and they fled from thence in masses to Poland and Lithuania.[1]

To the sixteenth century, when the population of the towns in Poland was still inconsiderable, and trade and industry were but little developed, the Polish kings, being anxious to encourage these branches of national economy, extended to the Jews their special protection. But with the growth and development of the Christian population of the towns the Jews were gradually driven from the pursuit of trade and the exercise of various crafts. With the organization of town municipalities and with the adoption by them of the Magdeburg Law, having for its object the establishment of exclusive privileges with regard to trade and handicrafts, we find frequent applications from various towns seeking to acquire for themselves special privileges, to the exclusion of the Jews in matters of trade and skilled labour.[2]

In this manner the Jews, expelled from towns and excluded from industrial occupations, had recourse to such pursuits as were not protected by any privileges : they became money-lenders, retailers of brandy and small agents, and transferred their

---
[1] Stobbe, Die Juden in Deutschland, Während, d Mittelalters, 1866, pp. 102-108.
[2] The so-called " Privilegia de non tolerandis Judæis."

activity from the towns to small hamlets and villages, which further provoked the hatred of the Christian population and led to the adoption of restrictive measures against them on the part of the Government.

In Lithuania the legal and social position of the Jews was more favourable. According to the investigation of Professor Bershadsky,[1] the Jews, prior to the establishment of the Uniat Church in Liublin, (1569) formed a class of freemen subject to the immediate jurisdiction of the great Prince and his constituted local authorities. The inviolability of life and property, religious freedom, the right of free locomotion, the unfettered pursuit of trade and industry were the privileges accorded to the Jews, and we in effect find that usury was not their only pursuit, but that they also were engaged in trade, industry and agriculture.[2] No narrow religious exclusiveness of race prevailed among them; their relations to the rest of the population, to other creeds and nationalities, were as to each other. The Christian tribunals enjoyed undoubted respect among them, and they had recourse to them in all their suits and contentions with Christians, and even with individuals of their own race. Nevertheless, the attitude of the urban classes (the burghers and

[1] Bershadsky, S. The Lithuanian Jews. The history of their juridical and social position in Lithuania, 1388, 1569. St. Petersburg, 1883.

[2] So early as 893, when the Jews first sought permission to settle in Poland, they endeavoured to obtain the allotment of vacant lands for agriculture and cattle breeding.

smaller nobles) was inimical, inasmuch as in the Jews they encountered dangerous rivals in trade and money dealings. When in 1566 the nobles were enabled to give expression to their wishes in the form of laws, they endeavoured to satisfy their feelings of animosity against the Jews by passing the following enactments : " Let no Jews dare to go about dressed in costly garments and decked in gold chains, and their wives in gold and silver. No Jew shall have his sword or sabre ornamented with silver ; let his dress be distinctive to all. They shall wear yellow hats or caps, and their wives head-dresses of yellow linen, so that all may distinguish a Christian from a Jew.

In the middle of the sixteenth century the power of the King began to decline, and that of the nobility to gain greater ascendancy. The Liublin Uniat converted all the noble proprietors of land, into independent sovereigns, and all power practically became concentrated exclusively in the hands of the landed aristocracy. The noble class freed itself from all taxation, and the mediæval idea began to prevail that the profession of arms was alone compatible with the dignity of nobility ; that commercial and industrial callings degrade a man of gentle birth, etc. The spread of luxury, the acquisition by the nobility of the fertile lands of the Ukraine, together with the growing distaste among this class for regular labour, gave rise to the creation of a class of servitors ready with their capital and labour to minister to the increasing requirements of the nobles; the enslavement of the peasantry spread wider and took deeper root, and the Jews became in the hands of the all-powerful lords the instruments for the despoilment of the enslaved peasantry. Churches as well as estates, were rented to them. The noble landlords sought to squeeze what they possibly could out of their serfs, among whom hatred of the Jews and their patrons steadily increased, and finally found expression in a series of popular outbursts known under the name of " Haidamachiny," or exploits of the Haidamaks.

With the decline of respect for judicial authority and administrative power, as also with the development of the rights of the strongest, the individual, finding his life, property, and interests in jeopardy, was compelled in self defence to screen himself behind some organized associations bound together by a community of interests. Thus fraternities, guilds and artisan corporations sprang into existence among the Christians. The first signs of exclusiveness began now to appear among the Jews, and their organizations for mutual support to spread. The Lithuanian Jews united themselves with those of Poland, and withdrew themselves within their own communities, adopting the same views as to the autonomy of their tribunals and administration that prevailed at an earlier period among their brethren in Poland. At the same time the joint responsibility towards the government in respect of taxes laid the first and chief foundation to the *Kahal*, or consistorial organization of the Jewish communities. Under the supremacy of the Polish nobility, Jewish isolation and exclusiveness grew more and more marked, and reached its apogee in the seventeenth century, when all Jewish individuality became merged in Jewish unification.

Although animosity towards the Jews continued to exist during the seventeenth and eighteenth centuries in Western European countries, it was nevertheless not accompanied by the same bloodshed and violence to which the Jews had been previously subjected. The intolerance shown towards them partook principally of a social economic character. At last towards the end of the eighteenth century the Jews were granted in France and Germany the same civil and political rights as were enjoyed by the rest of the population ; by degrees an equality of rights was also accorded to them in other Western European countries ; after which Jewish insulation and exclusiveness gradually disappeared, and the Jews amalgamating with the Christian races by community of interests, the character of their activity, even that of their lowest classes, improved at the same time considerably.

## CHAPTER II.

#### BRIEF HISTORICAL SKETCH OF RUSSIAN LEGISLATION RESPECTING THE JEWS.

ALMOST to the end of the last century Russian legislation with regard to the Jews partook of an extremely intolerant character; not only permanent residence in Russia was prohibited to Jews, but they were even not allowed to make any temporary stay in the country; those who were within its confines and would not embrace the orthodox Greek faith, were expelled across the frontier altogether. The chief cause of this hostility to the Jews proceeded from religious intolerance and a desire to shield the native Christian population from the influence of the Jewish religion, as is evidenced by the answer given in the middle of the sixteenth century by the Russian Government to the King of Poland in reply to his request that Jews should be allowed to enter Russia for purposes of trade : "It is not seemly that Jews should come to Russia because they pervert the Russians from Christianity[1]" etc. The same reasons formed the basis of subsequent legislation. According

[1] Bantysh-Kamensky. Correspondence between Russia and Poland. Proceedings of the Moscow Society of history and antiquities for 1858.

to the testimony of Mr. Varadinoff, the official historian of Russian administration, "the history of all the cases since 1649, involving Jewish religious matters, bears on it the stamp of mistrust to the followers of the law of Moses, because the Jews, by their false doctrines, convert to their faith not only Christians, but persons belonging to other religious persuasions; in consequence of this the civil rights of the Jews were more or less restricted, and their settlement in Russia was prohibited; they were also on several occasions entirely expelled across the Russian frontiers.[1] The code of Alexis Mikhailovitch provides punishment of death for the perversion of a Christian to the Jewish faith.[2] In 1676 Jews were prohibited from coming to Moscow from Smolensk, and in 1727 an order was promulgated to the effect that 'all Jews found to be residing in the Ukraine and in any Russian towns, shall be immediately expelled beyond the frontier and not be allowed under any circumstances to enter Russia;'" a proviso was at the same time made that before leaving the country they were to exchange all their gold and silver coins for copper money.[3] In 1742 another Ukaz was published for the expulsion of the Jews out of Russia ("of all Jews of whatsoever rank and condition") and for their non-admission in future

[1] Varadinoff. History of the Ministry of the Interior. Vol. I., part 2, p. 120.

[2] Observation No. 441, in continuation of Vol. I. of Code of Laws of Russian Empire.

[3] Observation No. 5063 in continuation of Vol. VII. of Code of Laws.

into Russia, with the exception of those who embraced the Greek orthodox religion.[1] In the following year the Empress Elizabeth recorded a minute in her own hand on a report presented to her by the Senate, recommending that Jews be allowed temporarily to visit Little Russia and Riga, "for the furtherance of the interests of the State and for the development of trade," to the following effect, that "she sought no gain at the hands of enemies of Christianity."[2] In these few words is expressed the whole spirit of the old Russian policy pursued towards the Jews. The religious intolerance of the Empress Elizabeth towards the race was evinced not only in general measures adopted against them, but likewise in particular cases; for instance, in that of the once famous Doctor Sanchez. Invited to Russia in 1731, he became Court Physician, chief of the medical branch of the army, and member of the Russian Academy of Sciences. In 1749, however, when the Empress discovered that he was of the Jewish faith, he was struck off the list Academicians and was obliged to leave the country. "Her Majesty," wrote Shuvaloff to Razumovsky, "has much regard for men of learning, and patronises the arts and sciences in a high degree, but she also desires that the members of her academy should be good Christians; she has learned, however, that Dr. Schansez does not belong to the number of these." Thus it was on account of his

---

[1] Observation No. 8673 in continuation of Vol. XI. of Code of Laws.
[2] Observation No. 8840 in continuation of Vol. XI. of Code of Laws.

Judaism, and not for political reasons, that he was deprived of his offices.[1]

In 1762, soon after the accession to the throne of the Empress Catherine II., when the Jewish question was again raised, and the Senate unanimously recognised the utility of admitting Jews into Russia, the Empress, in view of the agitation of the public mind then prevailing, ordered the matter to be deferred to a more convenient moment,[2] and in the same year re-enacted the former prohibition as regards the arrival and settlement of Jews in Russia. Exception to this was made in 1764 in favour of the Jews inhabiting the village of Vetka, in Lithuania, who had joined the Russian sect of Old Believers.[3] In another portion of her memoirs the Empress Catherine II. says with respect to the exclusion of Jews from Russia that "their admission into Russia might have occasioned much injury to our small tradesmen.[4]

Such were the relations to the Jews to the year 1772, *i.e.*, until the annexation to Russia of the so-called White Russian region (*Beloruski Krai*), and later, of other Polish-Lithuanian provinces, a con-

[1] How even people of the highest rank in Russia regarded the Jews may be seen from the following fact :—" In 1738, Mavra Egorovna Shuvaloff, reaching the town of Nejin, was very much surprised at the presence of many Jews there, and wrote to the Empress Elizabeth : 'The Jews are very numerous and I saw them, the dogs.'"—Russki Arkhiv, 1870, p. 280.

[2] Account by the Empress Catherine of her own reign. Russki Arkhiv, p. 492.

[3] Observervation Nos. 11,720-12,260 in continuation of Vol. XIV. of Code of Laws.

[4] The Zaria Journal, Vol. VI., "Catherine as an authoress."

siderable part of the population of which consisted of Jews. It was then no longer possible to deal with the Jews by expelling them across the frontier. Catherine II., being a pupil of the philosophers of the eighteenth century, difference of religious creed was a matter to which she personally attached but little importance; the policy of her Government consequently towards the Jews assumed a more tolerant character, particularly in view of the necessity of taking cognizance of the Jews inhabiting the newly acquired provinces.

In 1786 was promulgated the first law "respecting the protection of the rights of the Jews in Russia," and it was then that the well known principle was proclaimed that "everyone, irrespective of creed, shall enjoy under the laws all the advantages and privileges of his rank and condition."[1]

This theory, however, did not find application in practical life. Although by the law of 1786 the Jews were allowed freely to enroll themselves in the Trade and Burgher guilds, and to enjoy all the rights accorded to these classes, on an equality with other citizens, but the operation of this law did not extend beyond the limits assigned for the permanent residence of the Jews. In the Ukaz of 1791 it is directly stated "that Jews do not possess the right of inscribing themselves as merchants in the towns and sea ports of the empire, but are only allowed to enjoy the privileges of citizens and

[1] Observation No. 16,391 in continuation of Vol. XXII. of Code of Laws.

burghers in White Russia." At the same time this regulation was extended to the province of Ekaterinoslav and the country of the Taurida.[1] Later, in 1794 it was ordered that " double taxes, as compared with those imposed on Christian merchants and burghers, shall be levied on the Jews who may have taken advantage of the above permission."[2] The evident contradiction of the above cited edicts with the broad principle of equality " according to rank and condition, without difference of creed and race," clearly shows that this principle only existed on paper, and that the legislature, in all the practical measures adopted with reference to the Jews was actuated, by completely different motives, which were in reality founded on considerations of monopoly, intolerance, and narrow-minded utilitarianism. Owing to the predominance of these views, the chief basis of the *Kahal* or consistorial organization of the Jewish communities—the independent apportionment of taxes among themselves—remained unchanged; although officially the activity of the *consistoriums* was somewhat restricted, yet in consequence of the exclusive condition of the Jewish communities in point of taxation, the *consistoriums* continued in reality to exist, as is testified, among others, by Derjavin the poet, who was sent in the earlier part of the reign of the Emperor Paul to the country of White Russia to investigate the economic condition of the peasantry. In his memorandum he

---

[1] Observation No. 17,006 in continuation of Vol. XXIII. of Code of Laws.
[2] Observation No. 17,224 in continuation of Vol. XXIII. of Code of Laws.

says "they (the Jews) have *consistoriums*, which arbitrarily rule them. At the time of annexation of the White Russian country these institutions were suffered to remain in existence without any modification, solely, it must be supposed, on account of the convenience they presented for the collection of taxes. In these *consistoriums* all religious and civil matters are regulated and the allotment of Crown dues and imports for commercial requirements arranged." [1]

"During the reign of the Emperor Paul no important change in the condition of the Jews was made, with the exception of their being allowed to reside in the Province of Courland, where they had, however, been settled for more than 200 years. At this time was likewise reenacted the old law, imposing double taxes on the Jews; those Jews who refused to satisfy this exaction were allowed, on payment of three years' double taxes, to leave the empire, and those who after careful investigation proved unable to pay such three years' double taxes were ordered to be expelled across the frontier, without exacting such payment from them."

In 1800, however, a special regulation was issued to the effect that all Jews failing to pay three years' double taxes, instead of being sent out of the country, were to be sent for labour in the government mines.[2]

In 1804 was issued a new law concerning the Jews,

---

[1] Archives of historical and practical information respecting Russia. Kalacheff, Book 4, 1860.

[2] Observation No. 1,9409 in continuation of Vol. XXVI. of Code of Laws.

the provisions of which were recognized to be framed (as stated in the Ukaz which accompanied this enactment) " as much in a spirit of moderation and a sincere wish for the amelioration of the condition of the Jews, as in the true interests of the aboriginal population among whom the "Jews are allowed to live." The main features of this law consisted in the right accorded under it to the Jews to send their children to all the schools of the empire, and in the inducements held out with a view to their engaging in agricultural pursuits, and establishing manufactories, for which purposes such Jews who were not able to purchase or lease land from landowners, were allowed to settle on Crown lands, situated in those provinces in which the Jews were permitted to reside, as also in the province of Astrakhan and in the Caucasus. At the same time in paragraph 29 of this law, it was said that "when the Jews shall evince in agriculture, commerce, and manufacturing industry, diligence and application, the government will adopt the necessary measures for equalizing the taxes imposed on them with those levied on the other subjects of the empire." But together with these benevolent provisions, which were really "in consonance with a spirit of moderation and solicitude for the Jews." Article 34 of the law ordered the removal of all Jews from villages and hamlets into the towns. This measure was based on the assumption that the Jews wrought injury to agriculture and industrial trades by holding land on lease, farming dram shops and small wayside inns which was henceforth

c

strictly forbidden under the penalty of a fine from 100 to 200 roubles, and banishment to Siberia.

Landowners and police officials were also exposed to severe punishment for permitting Jews to farm roadside inns and dram houses and similar places. But these restrictions remained inoperative owing to the great difficulties which their enforcement encountered. This was reported by all the local authorities, and Count Kurakin, the Minister of the interior, submitted on the 23rd December, 1808, the substance of all these reports to the Emperor in a special memorandum. In it the following reasons were set forth which rendered the enforcement of Article 34 of the Law impossible: "Many hamlets figure only nominally under the denomination of towns, and Jews, if transferred thither, would find in such places no means of livelihood owing to the fact that no branches of town industry exist there. Government manufactories there are none in such localities, nor are any private industrial establishments to be found there. The Crown lands on which Jews could be settled are of very limited extent in the provinces assigned for the residence of the Jews; thus in the province of Grodno there are only 200 dessiatins of such land, and during the first year several hundred Jewish families notified their desire to occupy them for agricultural purposes. That the removal of the Jews from their present abodes would involve great expenditure, and could not be effected within a short period of time, in view of existing high prices for everything and the liability of the Jews to the payment of treble taxes which greatly burthens them."[1] On the strength of these representations, an Ukaz was issued on the 29th December, 1808, suspending the eviction of the Jews from villages until further orders, and in 1809 a special commission was appointed under the presidency of Privy Councillor Popoff for the elaboration of measures by means of which the Jews "might be restrained from pursuing their present sole occupation—that of retailing corn brandy in villages—and induced to gain their livelihood by labour," and the Ukaz further stated that "the impossibility of removing the Jews from their present locations arises only from their great poverty, which renders them incapable of supplying themselves with the necessary outfit for any new mode of life they might wish to adopt. At the same time the Government cannot undertake to settle them all in new places." The other members of the commission were the actual State Councillor, Alekseyeff; Kazodavleff, Assistant Minister of the Interior; Privy Councillor Count Pototsky, and State Councillor Drujinin.[2]

The results of the labours of this Commission, which sat three years, were embodied in an extensive report, dated the 17th February, 1812. As this document is not devoid of interest even in the present day, we shall here give a digest of it.

[1] Orshansky, J. Russian legislation in regard to the Jews. St. Petersburg, 1877, pp. 278-279.
[2] Observation No 23,435 in continuation of Vol. XXX. of Code of Laws.

Firstly, the Commission was of opinion that the impossibility of carrying the provisions of paragraph 34 of the Law of 1804, "did not arise from the obstinacy of the Jews and remissness of the authorities, but from the natural and political condition of those provinces to which the residence of the Jews is restricted." The report then states that while the Jews retained their political independence and lived in their own country, they were an agricultural people. Subsequently when they were dispersed over the whole world, and everywhere subjected to the bitterest persecution, unrecognised as regular citizens of the countries in which they were domiciled, agriculture became to them an inaccessible pursuit. They were thus necessarily obliged to have recourse to trade as the sole means of occupation according with their new condition of life. In Poland the Jews were so numerous that the pursuit of trade alone was insufficient for their subsistence. On the other hand, the Polish landlords, owing to constant wars and internal strife, were not able to manage their own estates in a proper manner. They were, therefore, obliged to seek special means for increasing the revenue of their properties, for instance, by distilling brandy, lease of farms, etc. The correlation of these two causes led to the utilization of the Jews by the landed proprietors in their domestic concerns. The Jews became indispensable to the landed proprietors, and as they did not possess the right to acquire land and engage in agriculture, they were obliged, while residing in villages, to confine themselves to a retail sale of spirits as a main pursuit. When White-Russia was annexed to Russia, the Russian Government recognised all the previously existing rights of the Jews. The Ukaz of the Senate of 1786 confirmed their right of residence in provincial districts and their faculty of holding estates on lease. Thus it was until 1804, when orders were issued for the eviction of the Jews from villages. The immediate object of this law was the suppression of drunkenness among the rural population. The distillation of brandy, however, is a privilege of all landed proprietors, and forms a necessary adjunct to the process of agriculture. With the departure of the Jews, the retail sale of spirits would be carried on by tapsters of the native rural class, so that drunkenness would not diminish, but only a decrease would take place in the number of agriculturists. A peasant had previously been in the habit of selling his corn on the spot to a Jew, but now he was obliged to proceed to the nearest town, at a loss of time and labour, to sell his produce to a Jew, and the money realised he would still spend on brandy bought from the same Jew. The same result would ensue in the purchase by the peasant of articles required by him, such as iron, salt, etc. The commission also found it unadvisable to allow the Jews to reside in villages under the prohibition of their not engaging in the retail sale of brandy; this opinion was founded on the following considerations: The Jews who inhabit villages belong to the poorest class, and if not allowed to sell spirits they would be deprived of all means of subsistence. The poverty of the peasantry of White Russia is not caused by the Jews, and this is proved by the fact that there are also many Jews in the South Western provinces, yet the peasantry there are in a more prosperous condition than those populating White Russia. So long as the landlords of this latter region continue to adhere to their present system of working their estates, which encourages drunkenness, the evil will spread, be the village tapster who he may, either Jew or native peasant. This is confirmed by the example of the provinces of Petersburg, Livonia and Esthonia, where there are no Jews, and yet drunkenness is very prevalent. Should the Government adopt the proper measures for making the sale of brandy less lucrative, the Jews would be obliged to turn to other pursuits, perhaps to those of husbandry, especially if they be accorded the right of purchasing land. If the Jews be interdicted to sell brandy, such sale would be carried on by the peasants, who in order to increase their landlord's revenue will be obliged to do the same as the Jews. It should also be borne in mind that the Jews, with all their aptitude and experience in matters relating to the sale of spirits, never enriched themselves by this calling, but only earned enough for their subsistence. It would also be impossible to convert all Jews into traders and artisans; firstly because they would not find sufficient occupation in the towns and hamlets, where there is no demand for a great supply of services of this kind, and secondly because great injury would be inflicted on those Jews who are already engaged in these pursuits. As a matter of fact, the retail sale of spirits in the Western provinces is only carried on by those Jews who are unable to find any other means of existence. The Jews adhere to their present occupations because, owing to the want of means, the Government are unable to effect any radical change in their condition. Lastly, the Commission arrived at the conclusion that it was necessary to rescind entirely paragraph 34 of the Law of 1804.[1]

This paragraph, however, was not cancelled by legislative procedure, although it remained practically inoperative throughout the reign of Alexander the First; at a later period it was taken advantage of and applied in cases whenever it was thought necessary to expel the Jews from a certain province or town. In consequence of this, the position of the Jews became very unstable and uncertain, so that they lived in daily fear of being driven away from their places of abode. These apprehensions were all the more founded in view of the jealousy and animosity evinced towards the Jews by town communities, who frequently petitioned the government for the expulsion of the Jews from their midst. Such a petition was received in 1810 from the burghers of Kieff, who alleged that it was necessary

[1] Orshansky. J. Russian legislation respecting the Jews. St. Petersburg, 1877 ; pp. 280-284.

to expel the Jews for the preservation of the ancient privileges of the town, under which it was forbidden to all persons of this race to enroll themselves as burghers thereof, and to reside and trade therein ; also with a view to the suppression of the disorders, litigations, and disputes engendered by them.[1] This request, however, was refused on the following grounds: The Jews, it was replied, " began to settle in Kieff by general permission in 1794, and in 1801 an Imperial order was issued prohibiting their expulsion from that town. Consequently the presence of the Jews in Kieff has been legally tolerated for more than fifteen years, and their ejection would be attended with dire ruin to them. Moreover, by law, towns are assigned to them as places of residence, and not villages, where their presence is not of such beneficial effect. If some of their body do create disorders by their mode of life and occupation, in such case it is the duty of the local authorities to suppress all disturbances by legal means."[2] But in the succeeding reign, when the internal policy of the government was very hostile to the Jews, the citizens of Kieff renewed their application for the expulsion of the Jews from their town, and on this occasion they attained their object.

In 1827 an Ukaz was issued enjoining the removal of the Jews from Kieff. According to the testimony of Juravsky, the well known historian of the province

---

[1] Orshansky, J., Russian legislation respecting the Jews, St. Petersburg, 1877, pp. 280-284.
[2] Observation No. 24,098 in continuation of Code of Law, Vol. XXXI.

of Kieff, "jealousy of the Christian traders was the main cause of their frequent expulsion from this town."[1] The justice of this conclusion is confirmed by official documents. As the Ukaz of 1827 could not be carried into execution owing to the great obstacles it encountered, and when in 1833 this question was again raised, General Levashoff, Military Governor of Kieff, reported that in his opinion he considered " it desirable on the ground of public utility to allow the Jews to remain in Kieff, where, by the simplicity and moderation of their mode of life, they are able to sell commodities at a cheap rate." His Excellency further stated that " it may positively be asserted that their expulsion would not only lead to an enhancement of prices of many products and articles, but that it will not be possible to obtain these at all. Under these circumstances the interests of the mass of the inhabitants must be preferred to the personal advantages which the Christian trading class would derive by the ejection of the Jews."[2]

Petitions were also presented from other towns, seeking the deportation of the Jews, and these demands were mostly based on ancient Polish and Lithuanian privileges.

Thus in 1829, and on many subsequent occasions, the government had under examination various petitions from merchants and burghers of the Baltic provinces, praying for the diminution of the number

---

[1] Statistical description of the Province of Kieff, Vol. 1, p. 261.
[2] Observation, No. 6,418, in continuation of Code of Laws, Vol. VIII.

of Jews, and an interdiction for them to reside and trade in certain towns.¹ Many of these petitions met with success, and the residence of Jews in the Baltic provinces was restricted by various regulations which partly remain in force even to the present day.

In 1833 the inhabitants of the town of Kamenets-Podolsk also petitioned for the removal of the Jews from their town, on the strength of Polish privileges, granted in 1594.²

The Karaim Jews of the town of Trok, in the province of Vilna, urged their privileges in 1829, and succeeded in obtaining the expulsion of the Jews from their town.³

In 1838, in Wilna, the old privileges were re-established, prohibiting the Jews from residing in the best part of the town.⁴

In 1846 the guild of blacksmiths of the town of Jitomir complained of the injury inflicted by the Jews on their calling. The Provincial Chamber of Administration, finding that the Jews, although they paid the established guild dues and worked expertly, yet that they did not possess master blacksmiths' licences, attesting their efficiency, prohibited them from pursuing their craft. This decision, however, was rescinded by the Governor General, who found it prejudicial to the interests of

---

[1] Observation 2,884 in continuation of Code of Laws, Vol. IV.

[2] Observation 5,950 in continuation of Code of Laws, Vol. VIII.

[3] Observations 3,136 to Vol. IV., and 9,625 to Vol. XI., in continuation of Code of Laws.

[4] Observation 10,908 to Vol. XIII. in continuation of Code of Laws.

the inhabitants at large, seeing that the number of Christians who worked as blacksmiths in the town was very inconsiderable.[1]

The Christian community of the town of Knyshin (province of Grodno), taking their stand on the privileges granted to that town by the Polish Government, petitioned the local authorities to prohibit the Jews of the place from acquiring immovable property and engaging in industrial pursuits in that town; and in 1845 an order, sanctioned by the Emperor, was issued to the effect that all Jews who had come to Knyshin from other parts of the country were to be expelled from thence. Subsequently the Christian community discovered that the presence of the Jews in their town was beneficial to themselves, and they then, of their own accord, petitioned for the revocation of the previous Order, which was accordingly annulled in 1858.[2]

In 1836 a measure was adopted, prohibiting the retail sale of spirits by Jews in villages belonging to landed proprietors in the Novorossiisk region and in Bessarabia; this interdiction was called forth by a series of appeals to the Excise Administration of Novorossiisk by the brandy farmers in general, who complained that the activity of the Jews was baneful to their particular interests.[3]

[1] Observation 21,021 to Vol. XXI. in continuation of Code of Laws.

[2] Observation No. 32,721 and addendum to continuation of Vol. XXIII. of Code of Laws.

[3] Observation 10,012 in continuation of Vol. XII. of Code of Laws.

We suppose that the cases above cited sufficiently show the degree of social-economical toleration extended to the Jews by the inhabitants of the towns. Thus we find on the one hand the Government and proprietors of estates striving to eject the Jews out of villages and hamlets, and on the other, efforts made by the urban classes to drive them out of the towns, the latter in many cases successfully attaining their object. Under such circumstances it was difficult to arrive at any fixed results. An issue out of the dilemma was apparently discovered in an attempt to encourage the Jews to adopt agriculture as a means of livelihood, with which object, and in conformity with the law of 1804, about 30,000 dessiatins (81,000 acres) of crown land were allotted to them; this land, however, was not situated in provinces adjoining those parts of the country in which Jews could legally reside, but in the distant and almost unpopulated Novorossiisk region, to which consequently they could not, owing to its inaccessibility easily transfer themselves and their belongings. In 1806 many Jews, who had evinced a desire to take to agricultural pursuits, settled on these lands, and in 1810, 600 Jewish families, numbering 3,640 persons, of both sexes, were transferred to the province of Kherson (region of Novorossiisk); with this, however, the scheme of settlement terminated, for in the same year the Governor of Kherson reported that the "mortality among the settlers was very great, and that no more Jews must be sent to the province."

And, in reality, the position of the first Jewish colonists, who belonged chiefly to the most destitute members of the Jewish communities, was most deplorable. Physically weak, exhausted by preceding privations, and the hardships of protracted travel, and completely ignorant of agriculture, they reached a country almost devoid of population, and the virgin soil of which, for its cultivation, demanded severe labour and a knowledge of agriculture. To these were added other drawbacks; the new colonists were unaccustomed to the peculiarities of the climate; no habitations were provided for them; they lacked agricultural implements and farming stock; the failure of harvests was frequent, etc. At the same time the towns that were springing up on the Novorossiisk region (Odessa, Kherson, etc.), attracted the Jewish colonists to themselves, so that by degrees they became absorbed by these towns, which presented to them a wide and more congenial field for industrial and commercial activity.

In this manner, the first attempt at colonizing the Jews, with a view to training them to agriculture, was not attended with success. But the settlement of the Jews in the Novorossiisk region, suspended in 1810, was renewed in 1822 and continued to 1860 and a little later, until the government became convinced at last of the impracticability of the system of artificially converting the Jews into agriculturists by administrative rules and tutelage. Among the many causes, some of which have been already alluded to, that led to a failure of the Jewish colonies were the irksome rules established for their control, and founded on those introduced by Arakcheyeff in the Military Colonies of Norgorod. The numerous staff of functionaries, consisting mostly of retired military men, (officers and sergeants) devoted their energy not so much to the development of the prosperity of the colonies they were charged with administering, as to the furtherance of their own personal interests. But a very small portion of the enormous sums which were disbursed by the government for the requirements of the colonies were really devoted to the purpose intended. Out of 175 roubles allotted to each family for providing themselves with the necessary farming stock and implements, only 30 roubles were actually paid to them. The other portion of the money was employed by the administrative officials in building tenements for the colonists and purchasing agricultural implements, both of which proved worthless, so that the settlers were obliged to spend the 30 roubles given them in cash in repairing their houses and implements and were unable to procure other articles necessary for their own equipment. For the correction of the indolent, it was specially enacted that these should be subjected to the punishment of flogging and incarceration, while those who proved incorrigible were to be deported to Siberian settlements.

Such severity of rule and irksome administrative supervision, instead of proving beneficial, only checked the development of the colonies and made agriculture distasteful to all those who wished to engage in it. Lastly the distance of the points selected for colonization could likewise not conduce to the success of the scheme. [1]

[1] In illustration of what we have said respecting the establishment of the Jewish agricultural colonies we may here cite an official document on the subject extracted from the Archives of the Kherson—Bessarabian Board of Administration :—

"Previous to 1846 the colonization of Jews in the Province of Kherson fluctuated a great deal. In 1846 the Province of Ekaterinoslav was also assigned for future Jewish settlements, and it was contemplated to establish there 285 families from Vitebsk, who were willing to take to agriculture. The organisation of these colonies was entrusted by the committee of supervision to Stempel, the superintendent of the Mariupol and Berdicheff settlements, to whose control the colonies were to have been delivered not later than the 18th December, 1846. At this period however, no habitations for the new settlers had been erected. In colony No. 1, Stempel found only 10 huts, the walls of which consisted of interlaced lath-wood; two were in course of completion, and four had only been commenced. Stempel even then predicted that these hovels, built of frozen materials and during severe frost, by half frozen workmen, would fall to pieces during the summer heats and with the first winds. The Board, however, disregarded his warning, and continued to urge the completion of the buildings. By the 21st February, 1847, 117 houses were reported as finished; of these not one was really completed, and for 30 the corner posts had only been erected. The huts were small and so low that a man of average stature could not stand upright in the rooms. Moreover, the buildings had been built without any foundations, and on low lying ground, so that the damp must have inevitably struck into the walls. 'Similar buildings,' wrote Stempel to the committee, 'have probably never been erected for human beings, and as regards durability nothing worse could be constructed.' The committee, in their report to the minister, stated that some of the houses had fallen to pieces before they were occupied by the Jews, while others on official inspection were found to be in a state of decay. In this manner, instead of houses, which had cost the Government enormous sums, the Jews found only ruins, and at the same time the Provincial Board already accused the colonists of not keeping their tenements in good repair.

"'The cold, damp, autumnal air in these parts,' wrote Stempel to the committee on the 16th September, 1847, 'is already making itself felt, and in view of the existing epidemic may produce most disastrous effects

Some attempts were made to colonize the Jews even in Siberia. Thus in 1835, 15,154 dessiatins (about 41,000 acres) were allotted for the settlement of Jews in the Tobolsk and Ornsk provinces, and 1317 Jews migrated thither.

In 1837 13,336 dessiatins (about 35,000 acres) were allotted for the same purpose, and Jews began to flock thither in great numbers. In the same year, however, an Imperial order was issued prohibiting in future the settlement of Jews in Siberia, and those who were on their way thither were turned back and compelled to settle in the province of Kherson. Such rapid legislative changes, in connection with other unfavourable conditions, naturally paralyzed the benevolent intentions of the government for the development of agricultural pursuits among the Jews.[1]

among the Jews, who are housed in small damp buildings, and in some colonies they live in barns and similar structures, or almost in the open air.' Foreseeing the great hardships they would have to endure, the Jews sought permission to reconstruct the houses, themselves, but this was not granted them. Stempel then requested that the Jews might be allowed to pass the winter in the neighbouring villages ; this also was refused, and the Jews were ordered at once to occupy the houses prepared for them. According to Stempel the emigrants were driven with great cruelty out of the villages in which they had sought refuge. It is not difficult to conceive what the Jews suffered in their new abodes. Cold and dampness brought on scurvy among them. The walls of 83 houses consisted of thin lath-wood, which had become denuded by the falling off of the mud plastering ; in 23 houses the stoves collapsed ; in 18 the chimneys fell down ; in four the beams of the ceilings broke in two," etc. (Report of the 15th February, 1849, No. 116.)

[1] The following curious particulars relating to the settlement of Jews in Siberia are extracted from the Archives of the Ministry of Imperial domains : Benkendorff, chief of the " third, or political section of police," writes as follows to Count Kerseleff, Minister of the Imperial Domains: "It

As regards that portion of the law of 1804 which allowed the Jews to send their children to all schools, although in principle it may have possessed great signification among them, in practice it had no real import. For the Jewish masses, elementary education was requisite, as being more in accordance with their means and position; but there were at that time few primary schools in existence to which Jewish children could be sent to acquire a knowledge of the Russian language, without which, of course, they could not gain admittance to educational esta-

has reached the knowledge of the third section that some Courland Jews also proceeded as settlers to Siberia. It is reported that on the way they were treated with great cruelty by the officers and officials who accompanied them, and further, that on reaching their destination, they were not given the grain and cattle which they had been promised by the Government. The superior officials, also, did not extend to them the protection they were entitled to receive at their hands. Many members of the Jewish families died from the hardships of the journey; some perished from hunger; others were daily employed in interring their dead comrades. This news has produced such a terrifying effect among the Jews remaining in Courland, that no more will volunteer as settlers." The Emperor Nicholas instructed Count Vorontzoff, Governor-General of the Navorossiisk region, through Benkendorf, to 'institute the strictest enquiry in order that the guilty may be punished.' But this, of course, could not ameliorate the condition of the Jewish emigrants who were in a most doleful plight throughout the new settlement. The government suddenly found itself burdened with a great body of Jews stricken with sickness and disease, which threatened to become a source of infection to all the other inhabitants. In the documents here referred to, we find record of a series of measures adopted by the government to relieve the suffering Jews. The Governor of Poltava is ordered to provide the sick with everything necessary for their treatment, Hesse, the Vice-Governor of Kremenchug, to alleviate the distress of the Jews in that town. Hesse reports that he found 215 Jews in a building belonging to the town and called the "Sugar Factory," crowded together in a damp and fœtid atmosphere; sickness of every description prevailing among them; medical attendance they had none; and the danger of infection was great.

blishments of a higher class. In April, 1835, a new code of regulations was framed respecting the Jews which was in a manner a compendium of all the ordinances that had been hitherto issued separately on the subject. In the Imperial Ukaz promulgating these regulatious it was stated that "many special and separate regulations respecting the Jews had been issued," but that "owing to a want of uniformity of the principles on which they were founded, and the inconvenience that had consequently arisen in their application, it had been considered necessary to frame a new code of regulations which would embrace the rights and obligations of the Jews and harmonize them with those general exceptions of the law which it would be necessary to adopt." The principal object of the new code consisted " in a regulation of the position of the Jews which, while enabling them to earn their livelihood by agriculture and industrial occupations, as also to educate their children, would, at the same time, remove all inducements to indolence and illegal pursuits.

These regulations served as the chief foundation for the legislation now in force with reference to the Jews. From the sense of these enactments it would appear that according to the views of the legislature the Jews *per se* do not possess any of the rights inherent to all men and citizens; thus for instance, with regard to all Russian subjects, with the exception of Jews, the fundamental legal principle is that everything not prohibited by law is allowed; whereas for the Jews the maxim is that everything which is not positively allowed by law is to be considered prohibitory. Hence the necessity for the following provisions embodied in the code of regulations of 1835 :—" (2) The Jews while enjoying the general protection of the law, possess not only all the freedom appertaining to their personal *status*, but also that of legally acquiring property, pursuing agriculture, and engaging in trade, industrial concerns," etc. "(24) All Jews may at any time become agriculturists." " (104) Jewish children may be received as pupils in all the general schools, without any distinction being made between them and other children," etc. All these provisions show that from the legislator's point of view the Jews in Russia constitute an entirely exclusive class of people, and that as regards civil rights, they cannot be placed on an equality with the other subjects of the realm in a complete sense of the term. All Russian subjects enjoy the unlimited right of residing in every part of the empire. The Jews enjoy no such right. By paragraphs 3 and 4 of the regulations, the Jews are allotted a certain clearly defined portion of Russian territory for permanent abode, and this line of demarcation they cannot pass. This measure is apparently in contradiction with the alleged object of the regulations and is called forth by a desire to protect other parts of Russia against these "people who are more pernicious than useful to a State."[1]

Proceeding from this principle, The Code of Regu-

Observation 2,558 in continuation of Vol. III. of Code of Laws.

lations contains on the one hand a whole series of impossible limitations and restrictions with respect to the individual and social activity of the Jews, and on the other a string of measures having for their object the enlightenment of the race, principally by means of education and instruction in agricultural and industral pursuits. At the same time certain provisions of the code would seem to be based on the utilitarian ground of "deriving from the Jews as much advantage as possible to the State." We also find here an enactment which evidently proceeds from a desire to protect the Christians against the influences of the Jewish religion. It consists of a confirmation of the old law, according to which "it is forbidden to Jews to employ Christians for permanent domestic service." This restriction, emanating from religious intolerance, is at variance not only with the economical requirements of actual life, but also with the main objects of the legislative policy pursued with regard to the Jews. By compelling the Jews to employ in their domestic service individuals only of their own faith, the law encourages and confirms the estrangement and exclusion of the Jewish race, which on the contrary it should endeavour to counteract. The very existence of such a law necessarily tends to confirm the Jews in the opinion of their own alienation from Christian communities and compels them to retire more within themselves. By prohibiting Christians to serve Jews in any domestic capacity, the law deprives the State of a practical means for the russification of the Jewish masses. We know for instance that domestic servants exercise great influence in the matter of the acquisition of a language by children.

Although the capital penalties for infractions of this law were removed in 1865, the law itself, owing to an oversight of codification, forms at the present moment a portion of the Code of the Empire.

Generally speaking, the Code of Regulations of 1835, although framed on the strict principle of subordinating the life of the Jews to governmental supervision and control, at the same time by a whole series of provisions, creates out of the Jews exclusive and distinct communities with a consistorial organization, sanctioned by the State. Thus the regulations, while confining the Jews, as regards residence to the Western Province and New Russia (Sections 3 and 4) also prevents them from acquiring populated estates, employing Christian servants, and enjoins the inscription of every Jew in some Jewish town corporation, notwithstanding that he may be domiciled in a village or hamlet (Section 48). Rural Jewish agricultural communities must be established distinctly separate from rural communities of other creeds (Section 65). For the regulation of matters relating to the apportionment of taxes and other imposts to which the Jews are liable, the Jews select from three to five special deputies out of their own body who form the consistory (Section 66). The consistory enforces the regular payment by the members of the community of crown taxes and communal dues. It also has charge of the communal funds and controls their regular expenditure (Section 67). Rural communities and Jewish town bodies or guilds, apportion, by general arrangement among themselves, the amount of taxes due by them, in accordance with the position and means of each member (Section 82). In addition to the taxes and dues to which the whole population is liable, a special tax, called the "Korobotchny" is imposed on the Jews (Section 75). The Jews are bound to organise their own institutions for the relief of their sick and poor brethren. Provision is further made for the regulation of the spiritual affairs of the Jews, such as the establishment of synagogues, the election of rabbis, etc.

In order to have a complete conception of the legislative enactments, the tendency of which was to confirm the old alienation of the Jews from the Christians, it is necessary also to keep in view the special "Statute of 1827, respecting the recruitment and military service of Jews." This Statute specially defined the fulfilment of these duties towards the State by Jewish communities, separately from Christian bodies, and the control and responsibility of the due observance of this duty were imposed on the Jewish communities, which were thus armed with the power of delivering as soldiers, whenever they pleased, any Jews whose conduct was considered injurious to the interests of the communities. This supplied the consistories (Kahals) with the chief weapon by means of which they were able to suppress any attempts on the part of individual members of a community to free themselves from the control and guardianship of the consistories ; the result of this was closer union and solidarity among the Jews, and consequent increased estrangement from the Christian population.

Such was the result of legislative measures which tended to "derive as much advantage as possible from the Jews for the State," and to protect the Christian population against a race which was regarded as a pernicious one.

With respect to the educational provisions of the Code of Regulations of 1835, it must be doubted whether they could ever have been realised to any considerable extent. Although Jews who had been educated in the highest schools of the Empire, were allowed the privilege of entering the public service, yet they could only avail themselves of the right by special sanction of the Emperor, which was to be sought in each case.

The further development of Russian legislation with regard to the Jews to the year 1860 presents no changes in the Code of Regulations of 1835, with the exception of the law of the 20th April, 1843, which enjoins the removal of all Jews into the interior who were domiciled within a zone of 50 versts along the German and Austrian frontiers.[1] Although in 1844 an apparently important reform was introduced,

[1] Observation 16,767 in continuation of Vol. XVIII. of Code of Laws.

by which the Consistories were abolished, and the management of Jewish communities was transferred to the ordinary administrative institutions, the special taxes levied on Jews were however retained, and special Jewish bodies created for the collection of taxes and selection of recruits for the army among the Jews; moreover it was provided that special elders were to be appointed as tax collectors. In this manner the essential part of the matter remained unchanged, inasmuch as the chief cause of the isolation of the Jewish communities was not touched by this reform.

In succeeding decrees on the subject of the Jews, a narrow utilitarian spirit pervades them which becomes more and more dominant, as is apparent from a whole series of separate measures, the main principle of which seems to be "the acquisition of material benefits for the State from this race." With this object a certain extension of civil rights was made in favour of the Jews. Prior to this period, a utilitarian view of the Jewish question (in the sense of an observance of the interests of the state at the expense of the Jews) had prevailed on the part of Russian legislators; not unfrequently, however, such a view was superseded by considerations of religion and of class monopoly. Thus already in the eighteenth century when the admittance of Jews into Russia was characterized by religious intolerance, we find various administrative authorities urging the necessity of allowing Jews, even though temporarily, to take up their abode in Russia on the ground that such permission would conduce to the benefit of the natives;" that "their non-admission may occasion a loss of revenue to the crown, by a decrease of the tax levied on trade," or that "the commerce of Riga may be entirely destroyed, and there will be no one to sell the foreign goods imported." But all these utilitarian arguments had to give way before religious intolerance which prevailed at that time in the highest Russian administrative circles. With the annexation of the Polish-Lithuanian provinces to Russia, religious fanaticism began to recede before considerations of material benefit to the State, and these first found expression in the establishment of double taxes on Jews, and in the retention of the consistorial organization for facilitating the collection of taxes from the the Jewish communities and for enforcing a due discharge by the Jews of their responsibilities towards the state in the matter of military service. In some enactments relating to the civil rights of the Jews utilitarian conclusions of a social economical character are at this time also recorded. Thus for instance when on the 7th October, 1790, the Council of State considered the petition of the Jews to be allowed to inscribe themselves in the merchants' guilds of Moscow and Smolensk, the council adopting the opinion of Count Vorontzoff, President of the College of Commerce, decided that no visible benefit can be "derived by their admission to these guilds;" but that they could avail themselves of the rights of citizenship in White Russia, and that "this privilege might with advantage be extended to the Lieutenances of Ekaterinoslav and the Taurida."[1] This concession was made, it must be presumed, in consequence of the small population then existing in those regions.

In the Ukaz of the 29th July, 1827, it is stated, among other things that "the Jews cannot materially benefit the State," and that "the Government measures adopted *for deriving State advantages from this race* by the enactment of the special Regulations of 1804 for the administration of the Jews, and the contrivance of means for the transfer of Jews from villages to the towns have not as yet been attended with the desired success."

Permission to reside in certain towns and villages situated either within or without the limits assigned for the permanent abode of the Jews was frequently granted, or refused, according to the measure of their utility or otherwise. For instance, in 1819, Jew brandy distillers were allowed to reside in the interior provinces "until Russian master-distillers shall have perfected themselves in the art of distilling." This permission was given in consequence of the complaints of the local authorities (of the famous Speransky, from Penza, among the number), respecting the scarcity of distillers in these provinces. But in 1826 the further stay of Jew distillers in the interior of the country was forbidden, on the ground that "the number of Christian distillers there was already sufficient."

[1] Archives of the Council of the Empire, Vol. II., Part I., page 306.

In 1829 an ukaz was issued, ordering the removal of Jews from the towns of Sebastopol and Nikolaieff, in which their presence was found "inconvenient and baneful;" and in 1830, the local authorities experiencing some difficulty in carrying out this Ukaz, reported that "the Jews, who numbered 1115 persons of the male sex, had hitherto contributed their share in supplying soldiers' quarters, an exaction which forms a heavy burden to the town, and in discharging other general and local imposts; with the banishment of the Jews all the weight of these obligations and dues will fall on the Christian population, who will hardly be able to bear them, and, moreover, the town of Nikolaiff will be deprived of all its artificers, who consist principally of Jews."[1]

In the same year it was decreed to enroll as soldiers all Jews who did not pay their taxes (from the communities of Minsk, Grodno, Vilna and Podolia). This measure was based on the consideration that "the Treasury receives almost nothing from the Jews; whereas they constantly petition to be allowed to replace the recruits demanded of them by payments in money, which shows their ability to pay the taxes they endeavour to evade.["][2]

In 1834 an order was promulgated allowing Jews to keep small inns and to lease other property in villages, because if they were prohibited doing so "loss would be sustained by the Treasury," particu-

---

[1] Observation 3703, in continuation of Vol. V. of Code of Laws.
[2] Observation 3987, in continuation of Vol. V. of Code of Laws.

larly as a considerable class would be deterred from engaging in the farming of brandy, which pursuit the members of this class more particularly follow."[1]

In 1838 Jews were allowed to reside in the town of Novoalexandrovsk "in consequence of the small number of its inhabitants, and for the purpose of its extension."[2]

In 1843 the Jews were, by special decree, permitted to establish distilleries in towns, in consideration "of the possibility of a decrease in the yield of the excise dues should Jews be prohibited to distill brandy."[3]

In 1844, Jews of the skilled artisan class were allowed to settle along the eastern coast of the Black Sea, in consequence of the representations made by the Commander-in-Chief of the Caucasus respecting the utility of permitting such Jew workmen to reside there, their services being much required by the garrisons stationed along the Black Sea military coast line. Later in 1846, it was deemed expedient to allow Jew artificers to take up their abode in the seaport towns of the north eastern coast of the Black Sea "though only for a time, and with the proviso that Jews, under the guise of temporary residence, shall not form permanent settlements in those places."[4]

In the same year His Imperial Majesty confirmed

---

[1] Observation No. 17,645 in continuation of Vol. IX. of Code of Laws.
[2] Observation No. 11,200, in continuation of Vol. XIII. of Code of Laws.
[3] Observation No. 16,416, in continuation of Vol. XVIII. of Code of Laws.
Observation 20,707, in continuation of Vol. XXI. of Code of Laws.

a decision of the committee of ministers, permitting Jews to undertake by tender and contract the construction and repair of highways in villages situated in the provinces of Moghileff and Vitebsk (where Jews were not allowed to live), on the ground that it was not "desirable to divide the contracts for highways when these happened to pass through villages," and for the further reason that "owing to the scarcity in those parts of Christian skilled workmen, Jews chiefly secure the contracts." This permission, however, was granted subject to the stipulation that "they (the Jews) shall not permanently remain in these places after the completion of the work."[1]

In 1848 it was found both "useful and expedient to permit Jew traders to enter into contracts, also, beyond their residential legal limits, for the carriage of government stores, inasmuch as by excluding Jews from this kind of enterprise, there will be a decrease of competition among the competitors for these contracts, and the Government will accordingly be obliged to make payments in excess under them; besides, in many places none but Jew contractors can be got."[2] On the strength of these considerations a law was passed allowing Jews to contract for the transport of stores, etc., in places even where they were not allowed to reside.

"In 1851 it was enacted that in order to relieve as

[1] Observation 20,584, in continuation of Vol. XXI. of Code of Laws.
[2] Observation 25,726, in continuation of Vol. XXVI. of Code of Laws.

much as possible the nobility of Courland of the burdensome duty of maintaining the high roads in their province, Jews of the province of Kovno may, as requested by the above nobility, be employed for such work, on condition that they do not settle permanently in Courland after the expiration of the term of their engagement." [1]

Later legislation with regard to the Jews continues to be characterised by the predominance of the utilitarian principle. The most important laws passed during the last reign, with reference to an extension of the rights of the Jews, mostly owned their origin to considerations of State utility; this would appear to be the case from the circumstance that the enactments in question did not apply to the whole Jewish population, but only to certain categories of Jews whose activity was recognized as beneficial to the State.

Of this character were the well known laws of the 16th March, 1859; of the 27th November, 1861, and of the 28 June, 1865, permitting Jews of the first guild and Jew artificers to reside all over Russia, and also allowing Jews who have taken learned degrees to enter the public service "in all the departments of the State, without any limitations as to their places of abode."

With reference to the law of 1865, extending the residential rights of Jew artificers, direct official evidence is in existence, pointing to the extraordinary

[1] Observation 21,858, in continuation of Vol. XXIII. of Code of Laws.

scarcity of skilled labour in the provinces, outside the legal limit of Jewish domicile, and showing that this circumstance was the chief actuating cause of the issue of this law. Thus one of the considerations put forward by the Minister of the Interior in support of this measure was that "those provinces in which a scarcity of good workmen is felt, would be able to secure skilled artificers in the Jews." This is confirmed by the endeavours of the Kursk nobility, of the Governor of the province of Voronij and others to obtain the sanction of the government for allowing Jew artificers distillers and generally operatives, and skilled workmen to reside in the interior provinces of the empire; the Ministry of Finance deemed it necessary to satisfy these requests as it considered the success of the new system of taxation of spirituous liquors recently adopted by the government to be dependent on such permission."[1]

It is necessary, however, to observe that in addition to the purely utilitarian considerations which formed the basis of the law of 1865, other objects were also kept in view by this enactment, such as the improvement of the very unsatisfactory condition of the Jewish population within their limits of prescribed domicile, and the gradual fusion of the Jews with the native population of the Empire. According to the conclusions of the Ministry of Finances "the Jewish artisans crowded within the limited confines assigned for their permanent abode, and residing in

[1] Observation No. 42,264, in continuation of Vol. XI., of Code of Laws.

the midst of a poverty-stricken population, obtain employment at prices excessively low, to the injury of the durability and quality of their work, being only anxious that the price of the products of their skill should be accessible to the mass of consumers. The Christian workmen compete with them also in the same direction and at the same sacrifice, and this engenders an unhealthy emulation which injuriously affects the well-being of both. This circumstance in a great measure accounts for the arrears of taxation. Notwithstanding that the capitation tax was abolished in 1863 for the lower class of burghers, and that considerable sums were set apart from the 'Korobotchny' or special tax towards defraying the Crown dues of the Jews, yet the arrears of taxes owing by Jewish communities have not been paid to the present time." The Ministry was therefore of opinion that "the diminution of the number of Jewish artisans (within the reserved limits) would conduce to a more proportionate relation between the supply of skilled workmanship and its demand—a relation both necessary for the well-being of the former as in the interests of the latter. Moreover, if Jewish artificers were allowed to take up their abode in places to which they have now no legal access, and where they would constitute a considerable minority, entirely swamped by the native population, the national peculiarities of the race would all the sooner become effaced. That this effect would be thus produced is proved by the report of the

Governor of the province of Poltava, according to whose testimony there are fewer Jews in that province than in the western region, and the Jews in that part of the country have become completely amalgamated with the native population."[1]

In conclusion we may cite wider conception of the question by Count Strogonoff, former Governor-General of Bessarabia and of the Novorossiisk region, who says that "the existence at the present period of limitations of any kind of the civil rights of Jews, as compared with the Christian population, is not in consonance either with the spirit and tendencies of the times or with the efforts of the Government to effect a fusion of the Jews with the native population of the Empire," and he, therefore, would allow the Jews to reside in all the parts of the Empire and to engage, without limitations of any kind, and with the same rights as those possessed by all other Russian subjects, in every trade and calling selected by themselves according to their aptitude and idiosyncracy.[2]

But concurrently with the measures adopted for the gradual alleviation of the condition of the Jews within the territory to which their abode was confined, other enactments were passed restricting the sphere of the activity and rights of property of the Jews. For instance, according to the laws of the 5th March and 10th July, 1864, the Jews are forbidden to acquire

[1] Observation No. 42,264, in continuation of Vol. XI. of Code of Laws.
[2] Observation 42,264, in continuation of Vol. XI. of Code of Laws.

E

land in the western region, while the Russians who have become possessors on preferential and privileged conditions of estates in that quarter, are not allowed either to sell, let on lease, or entrust for management their estates to Jews ; "the latter may only be distillers and renters of village inns." [1]

Later, in 1867, it was found expedient to allow Jews to rent flour mills and factories situated on estates, as " no one but Jews could be found there to manage these mills and factories, such management requiring special technical knowledge and experience. Consequently, the prohibition against renting such places to Jews, places our Russian landowners in a very difficult position, and may even lead to the extinction of some mills and factories, a contingency which may prejudicially affect the industrial and agricultural interests of the region, as also the work of establishing Russian landlords in the western provinces."

From this concise historical sketch of Russian legislation respecting the Jews, it is evident that both in Russia and in Western Europe, the leading principle adopted to the end of the last century, in the treatment of the Jews was intolerance, founded partly on religious and partly on social-economical prejudices. The legislative enactments that were passed for the purpose of amalgamating the Jewish race with the aboriginal population, in most cases did not attain the

---

[1] Observations 40,656 and 41,039 in continuation of Vol. XXXIX. of Code of Laws.

intended object, these being paralysed by other measures based on totally different principles, and tending to increase the isolation and alienation of the Jews from the rest of the population. Religious intolerance, the encouragement of monopolistic tendencies of the Christian trading and industrial classes, the observance of the utilitarian-fiscal interests of the State, and the protection of the Christian population against the Jews by means of purely mechanical restrictions—such are the chief motives by which Russia has hitherto been actuated in its special legislation with regard to the Jews.

In this manner the Jewish question, owing to a complete disregard of objective treatment by the Russian Government, could not be correctly formulated, and consequently correctly solved—and the question remains an open one to the present day.

## CHAPTER III.

#### RUSSIAN LAWS IN OPERATION RESPECTING THE JEWS.

When examining the legal rights, or more correctly the disabilities of the Jews, it would be a great error to take alone into consideration the restrictions found in that portion of the Russian Code which specially refers to the Jews, *i.e.* those enactments of which the restrictive character is beyond all doubt.

In practice, the laws that have been passed with the object of placing the Jews on as much equality as possible with the Christians are rendered either partially inoperative, or nullified altogether, and reduced to a dead letter. It is difficult to say whether this proceeds from hereditary animosity entertained towards the Jews by the Russian administrators of the law, or arises from the ambiguity, contradiction and errors of codification in which the Russian Code abounds, especially the laws which regulate the position of the Jews; or lastly whether this partial application and nullification of the law in regard to the race, owe their origin to the principle which underlies all Russian legislation respecting the Jews, and according to which everything that is not sanctioned by law is prohibited. Probably it is due to a combination of these causes that the position of the Jews in Russia, is from a legal point of view in so unsatisfactory a condition.

In the present sketch of the laws in operation respecting the Jews, it will be necessary to refer not only to the actual restrictions laid down by law, but also to the limitations which find application in practice owing to the causes above referred to ; this is all the more necessary, as the revision and concordance of the laws affecting the Jews in Russia is now under the consideration of an Imperial Commission.

## LIMITATION OF RIGHTS OF RESIDENCE OF THE JEWS.

The centre of gravity of the legal system of restriction, with respect to the rights of the Jews lies in the limitation of their freedom of locomotion ; of the faculty of disposing of their labour, and offering their economic services there where a demand exists for them, and generally of their being deprived of the possibility of removing beyond the limits assigned for their permanent abode, where they are massed together on a comparatively small area, (Vide Part IV.) and where, owing to inordinate competition, they constitute an injurious element in the sphere of social economical industry.

Although by the laws of the 16th March, 1859, 27th November, 1861, the 28th July, 1865, and of the 19th January, 1879, the rights of residence are enlarged of certain classes of the Jewish population, namely of merchants of the first guild of persons who have gone through a course of instruction in the higher schools, and of artisans, by the permission accorded to them, to live in any part of the Empire they may choose ; but in reality this extension of privilege has remained inoperative and has not affected that portion of the Jewish masses which suffers most from its confined and restricted position. If some Jew merchants of the first guild have taken advantage of the right accorded them, very few Jews educated in the higher schools have done so, while as regards Jew artificers, the law of 1865 remains a dead letter.

According to the valuable ethnographical information collected in various places by officers of the general staff, and which has been embodied in a work of many volumes, bearing the title of "Materials Collected by Officers of the General Staff," it would appear that Jew merchants in general, and those of the first guild in particular, form a very insignificant portion of the Jewish population ; thus, for instance, in the province of Minsk, according to the tables of population drawn up by the Crown Chamber of Minsk by Ukaz, of the 22nd November, 1851, the proportion of merchants of all the three guilds is only 2.3 per 100 Jews.[1] The same ratio is likewise observable in the other provinces reserved for Jewish domicile. It must also be remembered that even among this insignificant number of Jew merchants, only a few have taken advantage of the ceded right of permanently residing in all parts of the Empire, because merchants of the first guild, for instance, possessing as they generally do,

[1] Description of the Province of Minsk, Vol. I., p. 659.

sufficient pecuniary means, do not suffer any inconvenience attending their residence within the limits prescribed by law for the abode of their poorer brethren, and consequently do not experience the necessity of a change of domicile. This right was equally valueless to those who had received high educations, in consequence of the actual inaccessibility to them of most of the branches of the public service. The law of 1861, which gave admission to the interior provinces, to all Jews who had passed through the higher schools, and who were, therefore, eligible for employment under the Government in all its departments, remained practically inoperative on account of the concluding proviso of the enactment.

To a still smaller degree did Jew artisans avail themselves of the benevolent law of the 25th July, 1865, which was to raise the well-being of a considerable portion of the Jewish masses. It will be necessary to dwell at greater length on this point, seeing that it is so frequently cited as a proof of the futility of abolishing the legal limits of Jewish domicile, which is alleged not to exercise any injurious influence over the economical condition of the Jewish population at large. When we closely examine the causes that chiefly rendered nugatory the practical application of the law of 1865, we find that the law itself contained the germs which reduced it in practice to an insignificant palliative measure. Firstly, according to the law of 1865, Jew artisans, on their settlement in the interior provinces, could not acquire there a fixed domicile, which would more or less have secured their permanent well-being; these artisans also did not possess the right of inscribing themselves as fixed inhabitants in their new places of abode, where they, therefore, appeared only as sojourners, inasmuch as they still remained under the complete arbitrary control of the Jewish communities of their original place of domicile situated within the prescribed limits of their original residence. By compelling these Jewish immigrants annually to obtain from the police authorities certificates of their trustworthiness, and from their communities a residential passport, the law paralysed to a considerable degree all desire on the part of the artisans to leave their original abodes, particularly as the slightest delay on the part of the communities in supplying the requisite passport, or the creation of any difficulties by the police authorities in the issue of the prescribed certificate of trustworthiness was sufficient to doom whole families to repatriation, as was frequently the case. This was one of the reasons why the migration of Jew artisans to the interior provinces did not attain any development, and why the law of 1865, which the Government hoped would have the effect of distributing a portion of the Jewish population over the interior portion of the country, did not produce the expected results. Another cause of failure, which did not arise from any part of its provisions, but which was caused, by its practical working, is to be attributed to the fact of the continued dependence of the Jew artisans on the Artisan guilds of those localites which the emigrants had chosen for their abode. After presenting to the police all the necessary documents, such as a passport, a diploma of the trade guild of the town from which the emigrant had come, a testimonial of trustworthiness and a certificate of the master-artificer with whom he had previously worked, the Jew settler had still to make application to the local guild to be tested as to his proficiency in the particular craft he followed ; and it was only after this that he received, or did not receive, permission to reside in the town he had selected for his new abode, according to the inclination or otherwise of the local guild. The third very material cause of the practically inoperative character of the laws of 1865 consisted in the apprehensions entertained by the authorities with regard to the circumstances in which a Jewish family would be placed in the event of the death of its head. The fact was, that according to Point 3 of the law of 1865 Jew artisans "when emigrating beyond the limits assigned for Jewish domicile are permitted to be accompanied by the members of their families, that is to say, by their wives, children and infant brothers and sisters." According to the sense of this proviso even the aged parents of the Jew artisan do not enjoy the right of following him, and the family, after the death of its head beyond the legal boundary of abode established for Jews, is generally forced to return to its original place of domicile. Lastly, according to the strict interpretation of the law, even Jew-artificers, when no longer physically capable of plying their trade, may be sent back from the localities in which they may have passed the greater portion of their lives to their long-abandoned original places of domicile, where even at a more vigorous period of their existence, they were unable to gain a livelihood.

But even all the enumerated hindrances do not exhaust the causes of the practically inoperative character of the law of 1865. We have only indicated those which arise from the very wording, so to say of the law. But in addition to these, there were other circumstances that exercised an unfavourable influence over the practical application of the law of 1865. Thus while with the promulgation of the law giving access to the interior provinces to the most industrious, though at the same time the poorest classes of the Jewish population, necessary measures were not adopted for affording pecuniary assistance for emigration, for instance, out of special Jewish funds, to those desirous of leaving their homes. To the failure of the law of 1865 contributed also to no small extent a natural distrust with regard to its force—a feeling inherent in the Jews in view of the spirit in which the laws concerning them were framed, as explained in the preceding chapter. This feeling of mistrust took deeper root in consequence of the irregular application and arbitrary interpretation of particular sections of the law, and the restriction of the trading rights of the artisan Jews founded on a departmental interpretation issued a year after the promulgation of the law. In general, it may be observed that " circular legislation," (departmental) always proceeded side by side with codified legislation, and it not unfrequently happened that a right established by the latter was nullified by the former, unexpectedly for those concerned.

Article 70 of the Code for the Prevention of Crime (Edition 1876) also contributed to the failure of the law of 1865. According to this Article the residence in any single locality of Sabbatarians, *i.e.*, of persons belonging to the so-called Judaical heresy, entails the expulsion from the whole district of all Jews settled within it.

It is also necessary to take into consideration the circumstance that a considerable portion of the Jewish population, although not belonging to any artificers' unions, was, nevertheless, engaged in some kind of productive labour, and completely exempt from the operation of the law of 1865, the sphere of application of which was, consequently, still further restricted.

We thus find that, in consequence of the unsatisfactory results of the operation of the law of 1865, the distressed economic condition of the Jewish masses was not improved, while increasing competition continued to drive the Jews from the sphere of productive labour to pursuits of a less useful nature. Under the category of limitations as to rights of residence must also be classed the prohibition against Jews settling within 50 versts of the German and Austrian frontiers. (Passport Regulations 923, Vol. IV., Edition of 1876 of Code of Laws.) With reference to this prohibition, it must be observed that the Ministry of Finances, which is most interested in the maintenance of this restriction, having for its object the reduction of smuggling, sought repeatedly to obtain its abrogation on the ground that it was both unnecessary and inefficacious."[1]

### RESTRICTIONS IMPOSED ON JEWS IN REGARD TO THEIR ECONOMIC ACTIVITY.

Besides a whole series of measures limiting the sphere of industrial activity of the Jews, there exists the restriction above referred to depriving them of the right of free residence, which in reality is the most serious and irksome of all the disabilities under which they labour, seeing that it affects nearly the whole mass of the Jewish population, while the other limitations only affect a class engaged in certain branches of industry. Of this character are the laws of the 10th July, 1864, and of the 23rd July, 1865, by which, on the one hand, it is forbidden to Jews to acquire lands in the north-western and south-western provinces, and on the other restrains Russian landowners from selling, leasing or entrusting for management their estates to Jews. According to the law of the 14th May, 1874, the rights of the Jews are also restricted with regard to the sale of spirits by the establishment of the rule in accordance with which Jews may engage in such sale only in their own houses. Lastly, the recently published so-called "Temporary Rules" may

[1] *Vide* "Materials for the organization of the condition of the Jews."

be said to crown the edifice of Jewish disabilities. By these rules, promulgated on the 3rd May, 1882, Jews are prohibited (1) to settle in future in villages and hamlets ; (2) to acquire immovable property, to hold on lease or manage the same outside the pale of towns, great and small. The operation of these rules extends to the whole of the Jewish population domiciled within the prescribed boundary.

As regards the exclusion of the Jews from rural agriculture by forbidding them to acquire and lease land, a measure which was called forth by political circumstances, it is difficult to understand why this restriction has not only been removed, but why it has received a wider development, notwithstanding that the futility of enactments of such a nature has been clearly proved. Moreover, the causes that necessitated its adoption have already ceased to exist in their original form. It must also be observed that the Russian Jews having no political centre of gravitation beyond their present country, where they have dwelt for several centuries, present a very trustworthy popular element in political respects. But if it has been found necessary to give this prohibition wider extension (since 1882) for the purpose of protecting the Russian peasantry, whose material interests might be prejudicially affected by the pursuit of agriculture and the hire of land by the Jews, then the prohibition in question should have been made to apply only to large land proprietors and lessees, while small parcels of land should have been exempt from the operation of the restriction, in order that Jews might enjoy the possibility of pursuing agriculture without prejudice to any one. In the present state of things, even those Jews who would wish to adopt husbandry as a calling are not able to do so. Lastly, the Jew agriculturists of the Novorossisk region, owing to the above restriction, are also deprived of the possibility of increasing their holdings of land with the assistance of the newly opened land banks.

But the above-named prohibition, even in the sense of a struggle against the principle of large estates, does not bear criticism. Once that it has been found necessary to oppose such a system of agriculture, it cannot be considered rational to place this purely economic question on a narrow social basis, more especially as under existing circumstances the Jews, who are *de jure*, excluded from participation in agricultural matters, exercise *de facto* in the western region, an immense influence over it, which is only natural in view of the low level of our economic development. This influence arises from money loans made by the Jews to land proprietors, and is also in a great measure due to the activity they exercise in the purchase and sale of agricultural produce, the transactions of this class being almost exclusively conducted by them, in their capacity of chief representatives of the trading class. In this manner the Jews, prohibited from possessing land, exercise great influence over agriculture, as purchasers of rural produce.

The power they thus enjoy over the population can

hardly be considered more useful and desirable than sanctioning their direct pursuit of agriculture. In the first case the Jews, confining themselves to an advance of capital to the producer, are enabled to live without labour on the proceeds of their loans, and by means of intermediary services, which in many cases are unnecessary and weigh heavily on the resources of the agricultural population. Furthermore, Jewish capital and Jewish activity finding no other outlet, are employed in trading transactions and feverish speculation in articles of local production, developing this speculation to an extent which does not correspond with the real requirements of the region. The result of this is an enhancement of the price of all rural products in consequence of their passing through the hands of so many middlemen. If, on the other hand, the Jews were allowed to engage in agriculture, a considerable portion of Jewish capital would be diverted to a productive object, and agriculture being thus freed from the dead weight of capital, would derive considerable benefit. The result of this would be a considerable improvement in the character of the labour and occupation of the Jews, who would accustom themselves to a laborious mode of life, and become at the same time interested in the maintenance and improvement of agricultural industry. It is also necessary to remember the well-established fact that, notwithstanding all prohibitions, many Jews, and undoubtedly the worst of the race, always succeed in evading these prohibitions by circuitous ways, having recourse to various shifts and expedients and to Christian substitutes. The effect of this appears in a demoralisation of a large class of individuals and a decline of respect for the power and justice of the law. It was the great Catherine who declared that "nothing so much enfeebles the laws as the possibility of their being craftily evaded. In the same manner unnecessary laws tend to dimish respect for those that are necessary."[1] The level of morality of the masses can be raised, not by repressive and restrictive measures, but only by altering those conditions of life which maintain and encourage this or that form of evil propensity of society, or of a certain portion of it. Many restrictive measures are adopted without proper heed being taken of the fact that, in combating a real or imaginary evil, one of still greater magnitude may be created, which will completely paralyse the effects expected from such measures.

The same may be said with respect to the other restriction imposed on the Jews in connection with the sale of spirit. The exclusion of the Jews from this branch of trade necessarily demands an extension of their sphere of activity in another direction, and as no provision has been made in this respect, it follows that the Jews, prohibited from selling spirits, are obliged to have recourse to less useful sources of profit, or to adopt expedients for continuing this sale by means of substitutes. The latter expedient neces-

---

[1] Instructions to the Commission for framing a Code of Laws. Page 423.

sarily increases the cost and risk of the enterprise, to the considerable disadvantage of the unfortunate consumer. The brandy question is essentially a general Russian question, and it should not be treated from a point of view affecting only one particular race. If complaints be raised against the Jews for encouraging inebriety among the peasantry, protestations can equally be made against Russian retailers of spirits, who as statistics prove, are more guilty than the Jews in this respect. Statistical returns of the yield to the State of the tax on spirits since the abolition of the system of brandy farming, show that in the provinces of Russia proper, this revenue has increased by 17 per cent., while in that part of the country situated within the boundary of domicle fixed for the Jews, the increase has only been 0·2 per cent ; that the quantity of spirits distilled in the former provinces has increased under the new excise system by more than 60 per cent., and in the latter localities only by 8 per cent., and that at the same time the number of distilleries in the first has multiplied by 45 per cent., and in the second decreased by 34 per cent. Generally speaking, the consumption of spirits in the purely Russian provinces has nearly doubled, while in the districts assigned for the residence of Jews it has diminished by 14 per cent.[1] In the period of 1874–1878, 36,415,893 vedros[2] of spirits were consumed within the provinces assigned for Jewish residence, which quantity, with a population

[1] Military Statistical Register, 1871. No. IV., pages 425-427.
[2] 1 vedro=2·707 gallons.

F

of 19,732,438 souls, gives only 36 vedros per 100 inhabitants. During the same period the quantity of spirits consumed in the provinces of Russia proper was 80,132,198 vedros, and this divided among a population of 41,339,040, gives a consumption of 38 vedros per 100 inhabitants.[1]

In connection with this subject we shall here give the interesting considerations and conclusions of the Imperial Commission, appointed for devising measures with a view to the diminution of the number of brandy shops in the province of Vilna, as also some comparative statistics adduced in support of the opinions put forward. The commissioners first unanimously report that drunkenness, in the sense of a widely spread national evil, does not exist in the province of Vilna, which is situated within the boundary of Jewish domicile. This assertion is based on the evidence of persons brought in close contact with the people, on data supplied by the district authorities, and on information derived from the local excise officers as to the consumption of spirits in the province. From this testimony, it would appear that from 30 to 36 million degrees of pure alcohol are annually consumed in the whole Vilna province, which gives an average of 27.68 per head, or a little more than five-sixths of a vedro of pure spirit. As a simple proof of the moderate use of spirits in the province, the commissioners cite the following figures of this consumption, as compared with other countries: in the

Annual of Ministry of Finances for 1876-1881.

United States it is more than 3 vedros per head; in France it is 2 vedros of spirits and 10 vedros of wine; in Hungary 1¼ vedro of spirits and 8 vedros of wine; in Germany, 1 vedro of spirits and 20 vedros of beer per head. Further, they declare that there is no such irregular consumption of spirits among the peasantry of Vilna, and generally by the labouring classes, as is perceptible in the provinces of Russia proper. It is to this comparative moderation that the commissioners attribute the punctual payment of taxes and communal imposts in the province.

The same conclusions were arrived at by the other commissions appointed to investigate the subject in the North Western region, consisting of the provinces of Kovna, Vitebsk, Minsk, and Moghilieff.

From the foregoing it will be seen that intemperance is less developed within the country of legal Jewish domicile than in the provinces of Russia proper, and that alcoholic excess is a common evil in the life of the Russian people. The causes therefore that tend to maintain it must be more general and lie deeper than those which are put forward by the advocates of restrictive measures against the Jews.

*Legislative restrictions applied to Jews as regards their admission to the Government and public services.*

Jews are prohibited from filling the public office of Mayor of a town and of elders of trade corporations; the number, also, of Jew jurymen in the Western region is limited to *one-tenth*, and the number of Jew municipal deputies to one-third of the general body of each respective category. The latter limitation is a very irksome one for the Jews in those localities in which they constitute the predominating element of the town population, as is the case for instance in the provinces of Moghileff Volhynia, Minsk, Podolia, Vitebsk, etc.[1]

According to the law of 1861 [2] those alone who have gone through a course of instruction in the higher educational institutions and received University degrees possess the right of entering the state service in all its branches. This privilege, however, is not accorded to such Jews who may have passed through one of the Universities only as "actual students," and recently in violation of the code of laws, the Ministry of War has established a normal standard of five per cent for Jewish candidates seeking admission to the military schools for training as surgeons and dressers. Reviewing all the considerations of a religious, economical, and political character on which the restrictive laws respecting the Jews have been based, it would appear that not one of these justifies the latter limitation. Russia has so recently issued from a war in which all her effective strength was severely tested, and the list of killed and wounded

[1] It may not be superfluous to mention here that when the question was raised of limiting the number of Jew jurymen, Count Pahlen, at that time Minister of Justice, strenuously opposed such a restriction, founding his objections on the fact that not a single case in the southern region had occurred in which Jew jurymen had abused the public trust.

[2] Recently, however, the ministry of public education issued a circular prohibiting the admission of Jews who had been educated in the higher schools, and who had obtained learned degrees as teachers, into the middle class schools, although the Karaim Jews, Mahomedans and members of other religious persuasions enjoy this privilege.

contains not a few Jewish names. We must also remember that this really severe trial did not reveal any such dereliction of duty on the part of Jew surgeons, as to justify any limitations of the sphere of their activity. Furthermore, Jew surgeons, as we know, are not engaged in despoiling any one, nor yet in any other baneful pursuit. If any Jew, or even Christian surgeons, be guilty of misconduct, the general laws in existence against crimes and misdemeanours and the rules for disciplinary punishment are sufficient to deal with any possible misconduct on their part.

With the exception of the limitations above cited for the entrance of Jews into the public service no others exist *de jure*. Nevertheless the service of the State is practically almost closed to them, as is proved by the fact that out of a population of three millions of Jews, which contributes a considerable percentage to the students of the primary, middle and higher scholastic institutions of the Empire, only about ten Jews figure on the list of officials of various Government departments (principally in the Ministry of Justice) and only one Jew military officer. The question then naturally arises is it possible that the Jewish race, the talent of which is undeniable, can be considered as unfitted for pedagogical, judicial, financial, administrative or other posts, irrespective of those of clerks, copyists, etc., in Government offices, which are similarly inaccessible to persons belonging to the Jewish faith.

Such is the effect in practice of that part of Russian legislation now in force which, assigns to the Jews the right of entering the service of the State.

In addition to the above, there still remains another class of restrictions affecting the Jews in respect of their activity and rights of residence. This particular category of prohibitions owes its origin either to a perverted interpretation of the laws or to the manner of application of such laws as have lost their juridical and practical meaning. If we consider the errors, contradictions and ambiguities of codification abounding in our extensive and voluminous legal code in general, and in the laws having special references to the Jews in particular, it then becomes plain that a wide field is afforded under such conditions for arbitrary interpretations of these laws. The cases of false exposition of the laws respecting the Jews are too varied and numerous to be considered at length, and we shall, therefore, confine ourselves to citing only a few instances. The regulations concerning Jew soldiers, who have either been placed on the reserve list of the army, or retired from it altogether, accord them the right of free residence throughout the Empire. After the promulgation in 1874 of the new code of military conscription and service, some commanders considered themselves justified in depriving the retired Jew soldiers of the privilege of unrestricted residence to which they were entitled under the regulations of 1867, on the ground that the new code of 1874 makes no mention of such right. Besides the apparent absurdity of this rendering of so equitable and good a law, which makes no exemptions in favour of the Jews, the forced interpretation is also refuted by that paragraph of the passport rules amended in 1870 and 1879, which declares as rescinded the prohibition that had previously been in force, forbidding Jew soldiers to reside in parts of the empire in which they could not become domiciled.

In violation also of that principle of justice, according to which in all doubtful cases the law must be interpreted in a lenient and most equitable sense,[1] some local authorities in the interior provinces occasion Jew artisans settling there no small molestation by arbitrarily classifying them according to the nature of their occupations; thus type-setters, lithographers, photographers (the latter, however, on the strength of a special circular issued respecting them in 1879), and persons engaged in machine work are, for some reason or other. considered as not possessing the right of residence in the interior provinces.

Such a narrow exposition of the laws concerning the Jews—an exposition which is inconsistent with their spirit — affects not individuals and families alone, but sometimes causes the complete ruin of entire Jewish communities. An instance of this kind arose only 3 or 4 years ago, when the Southern portion of Bessarabia was retroceded to Russia. By the law of the 27th October, 1858, Jews were prohibited from settling, after the promulgation of such law, within a distance of 50 verts from the new frontier. According to the legal axiom that no law should be retrospective

---

[1] "Semper in dubiis benigniora praeferenda sunt." L. 56, D. 50. Vol. XVII.

in its effect, one would suppose that the law of 1858, could not possibly apply to the Jews settled for centuries in the recovered district; nevertheless thousands of Jewish families were expelled out of it, beyond the prescribed limit of fifty verts from the frontier. It is not alone the old laws, the true signification and object of which have lapsed by the efflux of time, but also those of recent origin that are frequently subject to diversity of interpretation by various administrative institutions. For example the "Temporary Regulations" issued in 1882, forbidding the Jews to settle beyond towns and small townships afforded convenient pretexts for the expulsion of Jews by communial decrees from villages and hamlets, and these decrees were confirmed by the local administrative authorities. While residing in Kieff, cases of arbitrary interpretation of the law, in a sense unfavourable to the interests of the Jews, very frequently came under our notice. In many instances not only Jews of the second guild were expelled from that town, but also artisans, retired soldiers, and other Jews were so dealt with, who a distinct and positive law, (for some reason or other ignored by the administrative officials of Kieff or which was considered as inapplicable to that particular town), possessed the right of free residence throughout the empire. If certain classes of Jews are allowed free residence in the capitals without restriction as to particular quarters of the town, what foundation is there, we may ask, for any such limitation in Kieff, after the issue of the Regulation of the 28th

July, 1865, and of the two Ukazes of the Senate of the month of October 1871, concerning the rights of artisans and retired Jew soldiers? Lastly, Article 79 of the Fundamental Laws of the Empire, which is quoted in justification of the expulsion of the Jews from Kieff, or of the limitation of their right of residence to certain parts of the town, declares that a special law cannot be abrogated by the force of a general law, if it does not contain any provision for such abrogation. If such be the case, how was it that the general laws equalising the position of the Jews were abrogated by special enactments of a character similar to that of 1861?

We have hitherto referred to the restrictions imposed on the Jews with respect to their rights of residence which proceed from a false interpretation of the law. But even in those avocations which are legally sanctioned, and generally in all their trading and industrial pursuits, the Jews encounter no small number of restraints; to show this, it is sufficient to cite the recent persecution of Jew drug dispensers or chemists. According to the Imperial Order of the 19th January, 1879 (which has been embodied in the edition of 1881, in a note to Article 17, Vol. XIV. of the Code of Laws, Statutes relating to passports and vagrants), drug dispensers are, among other persons of the Jewish faith, allowed to reside throughout the Empire. Considering that by virtue of Article 952, of Vol. IX.; edition 1876, of the Code, all Russian Jews are subject to the operation of the general laws of the Empire in all cases which are not provided for by any particular or special enactment, it necessarily follows, that Jew drug dispensers were accorded the right of free residence in Russia for the sole purpose of exercising their profession. That this deduction is correct is confirmed by the circumstance, that neither in the medical statutes, nor in any other enactments of the Russian legislature, do we find any special rules for Jew druggists and chemists as regards the maintenance and management by them of dispensaries of drugs. Notwithstanding all the clearness of this proposition, an attempt was made to give such a meaning to the law of 1879 as would make it apply only to the free right of residence of Jew pharmacists and not to the exercise of their profession beyond the limits fixed for the domicile of Jews. In order to carry out this conclusion with consistency, it would likewise be necessary to deprive Jew doctors and lawyers of the right of pursuing their callings, especially seeing that the law of the 27th November, curiously enough, only provides "That they shall be allowed to reside permanently in all the provinces and regions of the Empire *for the purpose of engaging in trade and manufacturing industry.*"

In conclusion we must refer to the prohibition against the employment of Christian servants by Jews. This restriction proceeds from on oversight of codification and a consequent erroneous interpretation of the law. The real state of the case is this: according to the principles of criminal law, no act can be considered criminal if there be no law forbidding such act under certain penalties. Paragraph 2209 of the 10th Volume of the Code of Laws, forbidding Jews to employ Christian servants, has lost all juridical signification in consequence of the abrogration by the Council of the Empire (confirmed by the Emperor on the 27th December, 1865,) of sections 203 and 204 of the Code of Punishments, determining the punishments for its violation. Owing to this, we find that some administrative officials forbid the Jews to hold Christians in their service, while others do not. Some judicial functionaries take action on the reports of the police in reference to violations of article 2209, while others disregard them, on the ground that the law provides no punishment for this infraction.

Taking all the foregoing into consideration, we consider it superfluous to demonstrate that such a state of things is abnormal, and that it only weakens the authority of the law, irrespective of the evil influence it must inevitably exercise over the economical and social life of the country.

## CHAPTER IV

DENSITY OF JEWISH POPULATION AND ITS ECONOMIC CONDITION, WITHIN THE PROVINCES ASSIGNED FOR JEWISH DOMICILE.

Under existing economic conditions, the most considerable part of the population, consisting chiefly of inhabitants of towns, performs the functions of trade intermediaries between the producers and consumers of the products of labour. And as the numbers of the class of intermediaries should be in proportionate dependence on the demands of producers and consumers, it follows, as a matter of course, that a superabundance of the intermediary element disturbs the regular course of economic life, creates a proletarian class, unfitted for physical labour, and introduces demoralisation and dishonest practices into the sphere of intermediary activity, in consequence of which such services become burdensome to the whole population and excite a hostile feeling against middlemen of every description. Such a phenomenon is observable within the area of country to which the Jewish population is confined, where the proportion referred to is disturbed by the extreme density of the Jewish population. which is chiefly engaged in intermediary activity.

The excessive population of the country alloted for Jewish domicile is proved by the following figures supplied by the "Statistical Register" of the Ministry of the Interior. Adhering to the adopted division of Russia into so-called maritime basins, we find in the provinces of the southern portion of the Baltic basin (Vitebsk, Vilna, Kovno, Grodno, Suwalki, Lomja, Plotsk, Liublin, Warsaw, Petrokoff, Kalish, Kelets and Radom), containing an area of 5,085 square miles, a population of 9,577,013 inhabitants, of whom 1,216,856 are Jews, or 1,883 inhabitants per square mile, and six non-Jews to one Jew. In the 11 provinces of the northern and southern part of the Black Sea basin (Moghileff, Minsk, Tchernigoff, Poltava, Kieff, Volhynia, Podolia, Bessarabia, Kherson, Ekaterinoslav and the Taurida), containing 11,722 square miles, the population consists of 16,437,445 inhabitants, among whom there are 1,394,881 Jews, *i.e.*, 1,402 inhabitants per square mile and one Jew to ten non-Jews. In general, in all the provinces in which the Jews are allowed to reside, presenting an area of 16,807 square miles, with a population of 26,014,458 inhabitants, including 2,611,127 Jews, there are 1,584 human beings per square mile, and one Jew to nine persons of other creeds and nationalities.

In the provinces situated beyond the limit of Jewish domicile we encounter a comparatively sparse population. Thus, for instance, in the localities lying north of the Baltic basin, the population consists of 446 inhabitants per square mile, and one Jew to 326 non-Jews. In the five provinces of the northern part of the Black Sea basin there are 1154 inhabitants per square mile, and one Jew to 1625 non-Jews. In the nine provinces of the Caspian basin (along the Volga) we find 816 inhabitants per square mile, and one Jew to 2615 non-Jews. In the four provinces of the north-eastern portion of the empire, the population amounts to 473 inhabitants per square mile and one Jew to 4813 non-Jews. After this come in succession provinces in which the inhabitants are about 10 per square mile, with no Jews at all. The figures here cited show that the whole Jewish mass is concentrated chiefly within provinces which are already thickly populated. In some districts (that of Chaùsk, in the province of Moghileff, for instance,) the Jews form 50 per cent. of the whole population, and in many places there is one Jew artisan and one Jew tradesman to four non-Jews.

But by comparing only the non-Jewish with the Jewish population according to provinces and districts we cannot arrive at completely accurate conclusions, for the Jews, as is known, are chiefly concentrated in towns and small townships. "In the Western Region," say the compilers of the Statistical Tables, published by the Ministry of the Interior in 1863, "there are many townships the population of which consists principally of Jews and mainly of the poorest class." (Page 103.) We shall not take into account separate Jewish units scattered throughout villages and hamlets, inasmuch as they present an insignificant percentage of the whole mass of the Jewish population; and, moreover, many Jews have been obliged, in conformity with the Ukaz of the 3rd May, 1883, to migrate from villages and hamlets into the towns. Placing in juxtaposition the Jewish urban with the non-Jewish population in the provinces fixed for the legal settlement of the Jews, we find the following per centage relations : in the towns and townships of the province of Moghileff the Jews constitue 94 per cent. ; in the towns and townships of the province of Volhynia, 71 per cent. ; in those of Minsk, 69 per cent.; in Kovno, 68 per cent. ; Podolia, 62 per cent. ; Vitebsk, 61 per cent. ; Grodno, 60 per cent. ; Vilna, 56 per cent. ; Kieff, 49 per cent. ; Courland, 45 per cent. ; Poltava, 43 per cent. ; Bessarabia, 38 per cent. ; Chernigoff, 29 per cent. ; Kherson, 23 per cent. ; The Taurida, 19 per cent. ; and in those of Ekaterinoslav, 15 per cent.[1]

The area occupied by the towns, townships, burghs, suburbs, etc., together with the lands appertaining thereto, is as follows :—In the province of Bessarabia, out of a total area occupied by it 0·06 appertains to the area occupied by towns, etc., representing 39 square miles out of all the 659 occupied by the whole province ; in Vilna the relation is 0·29, or 223 square miles out of a total of 771 ; in Vitebsk, 0·07, or 57 square miles out of 819 ; in Voltynia, 0·20, or 260 square miles out of 1103 ; in Grodno, 0·15, or 105 square miles

---

[1] A comparison of the urban with the rural populations in the provinces " of legal domicile " with those of Russia proper gives very interesting results, which we shall present in a separate table. (*Vide* Appendix.)

out of 703 ; in Ekaterinoslav, 0·02, or 24 square miles out of 1229 ; in Kieff, 0·13, or 120 square miles out of 925 ; in Kovno, 0·23 or 170 square miles out of 741 ; in Minsk, 0·07, or 116 square miles out of 1659 ; in Moghileff, 0·12, or 104 square miles out of 872 ; in Podolia, 0·21, or 320 square miles out of 1526 ; in Poltavo, 0·11 or 126 square miles out of 904 ; in the Taurida, 0·04, or 41 square miles out of 1110 ; in Kherson, 0·08, or 103 square miles out of 1292 ; in Tcheringoff, 0·09, or 86 square miles out of 959.

In this manner all the town settlements of the enumerated provinces occupy an area of 1897 square miles. Taking into consideration that the urban non-Jewish population amounts in these provinces to 3,373.293 inhabitants, and the Jewish to 1,802,249, we find that the latter occupy 660 square miles, or 2730 Jews to one square mile.

Proceeding then to an examination of the economic condition of the Jewish masses, we cannot but arrive at the conclusion that the overcrowding of the Jews within the limits of their domicile, and the restrictions imposed on their pursuits could not possibly have conduced to the development of their prosperity.

The extreme poverty of the majority of the Jewish population is proved by official data, interspersed in the history of Russian legislation concerning the Jews, and by the evidence of various persons who have devoted their attention to an investigation of the condition of the population inhabiting the different provinces situated within the "limits of domicile."

So long ago as in the reign of the Emperor Paul, Derjavin, in his " Memorandum on the Economic Condition of White Russia," stated that the Jews of the lower classes, forming the majority of the Jewish population, " are in a state of extreme exhaustion and penury."[1] Subsequently, in the Ukaz of 1809, given to Popoff, when difficulties arose in the enforcement of paragraph 34 of the Regulations of 1804, respecting the expulsion of Jews from villages and hamlets, reference is made to the poverty of the Jews in the following terms: "The impossibility of carrying out this provision (expulsion of the Jews) proceeds principally from the poverty of the Jews, who consequently do not possess the means for leaving their present abodes and to settle down and establish themselves in the new mode of life they must adopt."[2] This poverty of the Jews was also repeatedly represented to the higher authorities by local officials and landowners, who urged the impossibility of transplanting a population of 60,000 Jews in consequence of their extreme indigence.

When in 1817 the Government, after the seventh census, proceeded to verify the number of additionally inscribed Jews, it was obliged to forego the fine of 500 roubles and other penalties to which the communities had become liable for not having entered such Jews on the registers, as also to remit all arrears of taxation due by them. The reason for this leniency

[1] *Vide* " Archives of Historical and Practical Information respecting Russia," by Kalacheff, 1860. Part 4.
[2] Observation No. 23,435, to Vol. XXX., in Continuation of Code of Laws.

was the extreme poverty of the Jewish communities, especially of those established in townships belonging to private proprietors, where, in addition to the Crown taxes, they were mulcted in imposts in favour of the landlords.[1] In the same year, a case of illegal possession by Jews of landed estates came before the Senate, and the necessity of evicting them was under consideration. Prince Galitzin, who was at that time Minister for Ecclesiastical Affairs, opposed the contemplated evictions on the ground that they might lead to the complete ruin of the Jews, "who were already in great indigence." On the same ground the Government, while constantly pursuing the Jews for the sale of spirits, was always loth to adopt measures to abolish this traffic and to expel the Jews out of villages and hamlets. Moreover, the ardent desire evinced by the Jews to settle in the Novorossiisk region, and even in Siberia (in the provinces of Omsk and Tobolsk) during the long period of encouragement of agriculture among them, tends to show how desperate was the condition of the Jewish masses, who were eager to abandon their miserable abodes and face hard physical labour in remote and, to them, unknown regions. Approaching the present period, there is no reason for supposing that the economic condition of the Jews has in any way improved. On the contrary, a whole series of causes which sprang into existence during preceding times, must have still further im-

---

[1] Observation No. 30,318, in continuation of Vol. XI. of Code of Laws

poverished the already lamentable economic condition of the Jewish masses, independently of the increase of the population that had taken place, and the consequent keener struggle for existence that must have ensued.

With the emancipation of the peasantry, the demand for the intermediary services of the Jews, who up to that period had been utilised both by the landlords and peasantry in the disposal of their agricultural products, considerably diminished. The rapid development of rail and steam communication also deprived the Jews of many means of livelihood, such as the transport of goods by road, maintenance of roadside inns and post stations, etc. The result of these innovations was a considerable reduction of the means of subsistence of the poorest classes of the Jewish population, and this reduction was all the more sensible, seeing that the Jews, confined to a fixed place of abode, could not easily find other employment.

From all the foregoing it is evident that the economic prosperity of the Jewish masses could not improve ; as a matter of fact they are in an extremely destitute condition, as is evidenced by official data and the investigations of many persons who have made the Western Region the subject of careful study.

In 1865 some governors of provinces reported with regard to the limitations of the rights of Jew artisans, as follows :

The Governors of Moghileff, Vitebsk and Minsk

said : "Jew master-artificers are not alone unable to exercise their skill, but from scarcity of work suffer great want, and when executing orders are obliged to have recourse to dishonest practices."

Prince Vassilchikoff, formerly Governor-General of Kieff and Podolia, explained that "in the towns of the Western Region, filled with Jews, artisans are numerous, and in consequence of excessive competition, they form a class of idlers. Deprived of all opportunities for honest labour they are ready to do anything to gain means for subsistence.

The Minister of the Interior in his report on this subject (condition of the artisan class) says : " the Jew artisans are crowded together in the places of their permanent settlement, in the midst of a poverty-stricken population ; and they undertake work at extremely low prices, to the detriment of the durability and finish of their workmanship, being only anxious that the price of their productions should make the latter accessible to the mass of consumers. The Christian artisans strive to attain the same object by the same means, and this gives rise between them and the Jews to an unhealthy rivalry which injuriously affects the well-being of both. The accumulation of arrears of taxes on the part of the Jews is mainly attributable to this circumstance ; notwithstanding that the poll tax on the petty burgher class was remitted in 1863, and that a considerable portion of the special Jew tax is annually set aside to meet the Crown imposts payable by the Jews, the arrears of taxes due by them remain unpaid to the present day."[1] This was the position of a considerable portion of the Jewish population, viz.: of the artisan class, until permission was granted them to reside throughout all the provinces of the empire; but as we have already seen they could not derive any advantage from this permission, and their condition was not ameliorated.

In addition to this, the now frequently recurring spoliation of Jewish property in many towns, and small townships, situated within the limits of legal Jewish domicile, contributes in no small degree to the final ruin of the Jewish masses, particularly as it is the poorest classes of this population who suffer most from these ravages.

In conclusion, we shall here submit some facts and statements relative to the economic condition of the Western region, and the persons who have supplied them cannot in any way be suspected of partiality to the Jews. The authorities we shall cite draw a most unattractive picture of the misery and indigence of the Jewish masses. This, for instance, is what Mr. Bobrovsky says respecting the condition of the Jews in the province of Grodno: "The most considerable portion of the population consists of the poorest classes. Being always in want, the Jews pass all their time in struggling for their daily bread. Encumbered with numerous families, they live in so crowded a state as to exceed all imagination. Not unfrequently a house of three or four rooms is occupied by 12 families. The exterior

[1] Observation No. 42,264 in continuation of Vol. XI. of Code of Laws.

of these houses is deplorable. Their interior uncleanliness extends also to the streets. It is sufficient to walk through the town in order to be aware of the quarters occupied by these unfortunate beings. The lives of the Jews of this class are passed in tribulation, want and constant bustle and agitation. Their fare is of the poorest; the daily meal of a whole family sometimes consists only of a pound of bread, a herring and a few onions. Their clothes are dirty and delapidated. For 15 copecks (3½d.) a Jew broker is ready to run about all day long."[1]

As regards the province of Kovno, Mr. Afanasieff wrote in 1861: "The Jews live in very crowded dwellings; not unfrequently several families occupy one room. Dirt, both internally and externally, forms a characteristic feature of their habitations. The more prosperous Jews have clean, separate rooms, decent furniture, some pictures, etc. The food of a Jew costs but little. In the morning it consists of bread with horseradish, onions, garlic or a herring. Those who can afford it, drink tea; their fare for dinner is generally soup with vegetables, meat or fish, with a similar meal in the evening. The families of some poor workmen fast all day long, and only get food in the evening, when the bread-winner brings home a portion of his daily earnings."[2]

According to the testimony of Mr Chubinsky, in the greater portion of the Western Region, "most of

[1] Statistical account of the Province of Grodno, 1865. Vol. I., p. 858.
[2] Statistical account of the Province of Grodno, p.p. 582-583.

the Jews live in great poverty and are very much crowded together; their existence is a constant struggle for their daily bread. The extreme poverty of the lower classes strikes the eye in all directions. Many are saved from starvation only by the help they afford each other, and the clanship that is so strongly developed among them"[1]

Concerning the position of the Jews in White Russia and Polesie (Minsk) we find in Mr. Zelensky's work the following evidence : "Half, if not three-quarters, of the Jewish population consists of individuals who might be accused of huckstering, brokering and idling, not because they are disinclined to hard work, but because these miserable creatures, intent only on securing their daily food, lead a hand-to-mouth existence without enjoying the possibility of occupying themselves in productive labour. These unfortunate families (undomiciled petty burghers) have neither stick nor home, live in the greatest squalor and dirt, uncertain, with all their desire for work, what the morrow may bring in the way of sustenance; and are almost compelled to have recourse to various dishonest expedients in order to satisfy their daily requirements."[2]

In the south-western parts of Russia, and in Little Russia, the material well-being of the Jewish population stood always higher than in the north-western

---

[1] Materials of the ethnographico statistical expedition to the Western Russian region, 1872. Vol. VII. pp. 22 and 210.

[2] Statistical account of the Province of Minsk, 1863: Vol. I., p. 659

provinces, owing to the fewer number of Jews who resided there, as also to more favourable natural conditions; yet even their condition was not much to be envied. This is what Funduklei says in his statistical description of the province of Kieff respecting the state of the Birdicheff Jews in the fourth decade of the present century: " There are no proper sanitary arrangements in Berdicheff in consequence of the poverty and dirty habits of the Jews. There are here about 500 families (nearly half of the Jewish population of the town) who live from day to day, trusting in providence. They are much crowded together, several families frequently occupying one or two rooms of a delapidated hovel, so that at night there is no vacant space between the sleepers. Many such dwellings are divided by a passage into several lodgings, in which the occupants have their workshops and ply their various callings, such as candle-making, tanning, beeswax refining, etc. Their families assist them in their labour and occupy the same dens, in the midst of malodorous materials and wares. In consequence of this, an offensive atmosphere pervades whole streets."[1] The same was said of Berdicheff by a correspondent of the "Moscow Gazette" in 1869: "In the parts occupied by the poorer classes of Jews the streets are only 1½ fathom wide; on both sides they are bordered by tumble-down houses, closely adjoining each other. Some of these dwellings are roofless; others have no

[1] Statistical description of the Province of Kieff by Funduklei. Vol. I., p. 435.

windows, while some houses have only three walls. In the open street and in the mud, troops of half-naked children are at play tumbling about among the numerous pigs."[1] All this refers to Berdicheff, which is considered the Jewish capital.

"In the province of Tchernigoff," says Mr. Domontovitch, "most of the Jews live in poverty and squalor. Their food is extremely coarse and scanty, and affords but little nutriment, consisting generally of soup, bread and vegetables, and it is only a little better on the Sabbath, according to the means of each family."[2]

The fact of the great poverty of the Jewish masses is proved by other phenomena of Jewish life which are the concomitants of indigence—disease and increased mortality.

Thus, it would appear from the statistical investigations of Mr. Zablotsky that the mortality among the Russian population within the limits of Jewish legal settlement during the period of 1844-1847 increased, as compared with the preceding four years (1840-1843), on an average by $17\frac{3}{4}$ per cent., while among the Jews it was augmented by 37 per cent., or by nearly half as much as the mortality among the Christians.[3] The indigence of the Jews is confirmed by the arrears of taxes due by the Jewish communities. In the province of Grodno the amount of these arrears owing by town inhabitants, mostly Jews, between 1843-1853 was

---

[1] "Moscow Gazette," 1869; Contemporary News, No. 38.

[2] Statistical account of the Province of Tchernigoff, 1865, page 541.

[3] Compendium of statistical information respecting Russia, 1865, Part I.

doubled.[1] In the province of Minsk, the arrears from the 1st January, 1860, were reckoned at 303,392 roubles of which 76,151 roubles, or one quarter, was due by Jews, the Jews forming at the same time one-twelfth of the registered population of this province, or together with the unregistered about one-sixth. It would also appear that in the same province among a registered Jewish population of 32,876 souls, 18,324 Jews, or more than half the Jewish population of Minsk,[2] were written off as incapable of bearing the burden of taxation, this number consisting of the decrepid, maimed, juvenile, absent, etc.

In the report of the Minister of the Interior for 1859 the explanation is afforded that "the irregular payment of taxes is caused by the poverty of the Jewish communities, and the comparatively greater amount of taxation to which they are made liable."[3] Although the figures above cited concerning the economic condition of the Jews mostly refer to a past period, but taking into consideration the natural increase of the population, and at the same time the diminution of its sources of subsistence, in consequence of general and local changes in the conditions of the economic life of the country, we can safely come to the conclusion that this condition has not improved; and our own

---

[1] Statistical description of the Government of Grodno, 1865, Vol. II., p. 753.

[2] Statistical description of the province of Minsk, by Zelensky, Vol. I., p. 66.

[3] Journal of the Ministry of the Interior for 1867, part 7.

personal observation of the life of the Jews within their confines of legal domicile, confirms this conclusion. This lamentable economic position in which the Jewish masses are placed, cannot but likewise exercise a most pernicious influence over their moral condition.

## CONCLUSION.

In conclusion, it is necessary to examine the grave, though somewhat exaggerated and yet not wholly unfounded, accusation which is brought against the Jews of preying upon the local population of the region. "All Jews are extortioners, and predatory instincts are innate in every Jew," is the sweeping denunciation frequently heard in society, and which also finds expression in a certain section of the Russian press. In support of the correctness of such an opinion, reference is generally made to the predilection of the Jews for a pedlar's trade and for brokery business. The circumstance, however, is lost out of sight that this tendency has been developed in the Jews by historical conditions over which they had no control, and which have extended over centuries; that a considerable number of the Jews follow industrial pursuits, and are engaged in physical labour having nothing in common with extortion;[1] and, lastly, that not all traders and intermediary agents can be classed

---

[1] Thus, for instance, in the three provinces of the south-western region (Podolia, Volhynia, and Kieff) the Jew artisans constitute 41 per cent. of the whole number of that class. Materials of the Ethnographical-Statistical Commission of the Western Russian Region, appointed by the Imperial Russian Geographical Society, St. Petersburg, 1872, Vol. VII., Page 199.

as extortioners, although it cannot be denied that under the present conditions of life of our peasantry, trading activity becomes one of the principal instruments for deriving undue advantage from fruits of popular toil and industry. The motto of the trading class always and everywhere is the same—" to buy as cheaply as possible and to sell at the highest price."— and it is very natural that traders should take advantage of every opportunity and endeavour to secure to themselves the greater portion of the profits from productions in the creation of which they took no immediate part. In this way the activity of every trading intermediary, to whatever nationality he may belong, resembles that of a parasite, and the rapacious habits of the trading class are not exclusively characteristic of the Jewish race, seeing that the same peculiarity is evinced by the same class of persons of other nationalities. In proof of this plenty of evidence could be produced if the phenomenon were not notorious. But although operations of trade cannot be considered as of a productive nature, as they do not call new wealth into existence, and are only carried on at the expense of producers and consumers, yet the services rendered by these operations to both producer and consumer constitute a necessary function in the social-economic life of a nation. To accuse the Jews, therefore, of preferring trade to any other productive labour, especially in view of the fact that many other branches of industry are closed to them, is, to say the least, strange. All free avocations or pursuits are called forth by the existence of a public demand. Free choice of this or that branch of activity, not prohibited by the laws, is the unalienable right of every person, who, in its selection, is naturally guided by his own inclinations and motives of personal gain, and not by official rules and regulations.

The question, therefore, to be considered is not whether the Jews are to be blamed or praised for engaging exclusively in trade, but what are the causes that so frequently convert trading industry into an instrument for fleecing the producing classes of the nation? The methods and means of sapping the vital forces of a people are very varied—but the soil on which the system is brought into operation and flourishes is always more or less the same. A state of economic depression and low intellectual development of the masses, the want of working capital and engines of labour experienced by the producers ; the absence of a cheap credit system, the prevalence of bribery, the arbitrary conduct of petty officials, and similar unseemly phenomena of our national life, place the labouring classes in a hopeless position, and force them into economic subservience to various intermediate agents and social vampires, who, being provided with money of their own (and with the means of obtaining more by means of credit), do not fail to take advantage of their position for preying on the labour and resources of the peasantry. This aspect of the Jewish question makes it part and parcel of the whole Russian economic problem, which can only be solved by a series of broad social-economic reforms directed towards raising the level of the well being and education of the masses. As regards repressive measures, they prove, as history and experience show, not only inefficacious in the solution of social-economic questions, but more frequently that they still further complicate these questions, and so retard their satisfactory solution.

For more than a century repressive and restrictive measures of every description have been adopted by our legislature in their endeavours to solve the Jewish question which, however, instead of approaching nearer to its solution, has, within the last ten years, entered into a more acute phase.

The legislative activity of the last reign seemed at one time to be directed towards enfranchising reforms which also embraced the Jews, but after taking one vacillating step in advance by extending the civil rights of some Jewish classes, it halted midway. The mass of the Jewish population continues to be confined, as before, to the "limits of settlement," and the limitations in regard to Jewish activity have received still further development by virtue of recent enactments. But we may ask who has benefited by these repressions and restrictions of the rights of the Jews? Has the national and economic antagonism which subsists between the Jews and the rest of the population been at all diminished by these measures? Has the economic supremacy of the Jewish element in the Western region been weakened, and has its population been protected against so-called Jewish extortion? The most eloquent answer to all these questions is afforded by the periodically recurring anti-Jewish tumults in the South of Russia, which clearly demonstrate the inefficacy of the measures hitherto enforced for establishing normal relations between the Jews and the aboriginal population of the region—and that no prohibitions and limitations of the rights of the Jews could defend either the native population against Jewish extortion, or the Jews against violence and spoliation, nor yet the country from the loss of millions of money, and the demoralising effects of mob turbulence. A congenial soil for the fermentation of anti-Jewish disturbances in Russia was afforded by the inimical and contemptuous spirit (transmitted for many generations) displayed towards the Jews by the native population, and which is maintained by the exclusive position of the Jews in the matter of civil rights. Their disabilities in this respect afford on the one hand, a very lucrative source of revenue to petty officials, and on the other, inflict a heavy burden both on the Jews and on the territory they inhabit. The existing inequality of civil *status*, and the overcrowding of the Jewish masses within the limits of country assigned for their domicile, impelling them to engage in unproductive pursuits at the expense of the agricultural population, not only militates against the improvement of the relations between the Jews and the other inhabitants, but also increases and renders more acute the traditional prejudices of the latter.

To attribute the existing evil—whether it be

Jewish extortion or Russian exacting rapacity—to certain national peculiarities is to divert attention from the true sources of the mischief which spring from the conditions of life of the labouring classes. If the soil that nourishes the evil be removed, the evil itself must vanish. If there be among the Jews, as among other races, a certain number of individuals of vicious and anti-social tendencies, it does not follow that all Jews are equally bad. Nevertheless a sweeping generalization is but too frequently applied to the Jews who are all stigmatised in one of our legislative enactments as persons " more harmful than useful to the state."[1]

In view of the marked disfavour with which the Jews are regarded by the Russian legislature, the slightest cause is sometimes sufficient to expose them to outbreaks of violence on the part of the hostile masses, who are not able to understand the true economic forces at work which so disastrously affect their well-being. It is, therefore, no matter of surprise that anti-Jewish riots occurred in many places in consequence of the circulation among the people of the most ridiculous rumours respecting some "Imperial Charters" and "Ukazes," ordering the destruction of Jewish property. These reports (evidently spread by designing persons with mercenary and other objects) were remarkable for the persistency with which they were maintained; they spread rapidly and arose simultaneously at points distant from each other in

[1] Observation No. 2558, in continuation of Code of Laws, Vol. III.

the southern provinces, and the people were so thoroughly convinced of the real existence of these "charters" and "ukazes" that no assurances to the contrary on the part of the authorities and clergy could shake them in their belief. It was under the influence of these absurd rumours that popular risings against the Jews took place. Wheresoever the reports found a favourable soil in local racial relations, the movement assumed the form of an economic struggle and served as a pretext for attacking the Jews on the ground of their parasitical and predatory activity; but in places where these conditions were absent, as for instance in agricultural colonies, where the Jews pursued their avocations in peace and friendship with the Christians, the agitation was altogether of a special character, and owed its origin entirely to the rumours of the alleged issue of certain "ukazes."

As regards the movement in such important centres of trade and industry as Odessa, Kieff, Rostoff on the Don, etc., it found in these places a still more favourable soil, firstly because a considerable portion of the population of these towns consists of trading and industrial classes inimically disposed towards the Jews for their very dangerous rivalry in almost every branch of trade and industry; secondly because there are always found in such centres not a few dangerous characters eager to appropriate the property of others, while the labouring population, drawn mostly from various parts of the empire, is distinguished for its turbulent instincts and for its readiness to manifest them in some form or other. The humiliated and despised Jews represent an element of the population on which feelings of accumulated discontent arising from particular causes can be most conveniently vented without the risk of encountering an opposition on the part of the victims, or remontrances from the other classes, who generally treat such outrages, if not with sympathy, then with indifference. It is otherwise difficult to conceive how in towns with populations exceeding one hundred thousand souls, an insignificant number of men, generally a few hundreds, could indulge in violence of the most outrageous character. If the enmity of the trading and industrial classes towards the Jews be not the chief cause of the anti-Jewish movement in towns, in any case it affords the movement considerable moral support.

The superiority of the Jews in the sphere of trade and industry creates a feeling of animosity towards them among the class engaged in trade, and affords ground for the accusation that they have monopolized all the trade of the Western provinces. How does this superiority arise? Reference is frequently made to the malpractices of the Jews in their commercial and industrial operations. That they have recourse to these expedients or plainly speaking, to dishonesty in every form cannot be denied, as is equally undeniable the Russian proverb "no cheating no sale," in which is expressed the main principle of so called "commercial morality," equally professed by a considerable portion of the commercial classes, without distinction of nationality. "Expedients of every kind and shades, from innocent deceptions to anything you please, excepting open robbery," says Herbert Spencer, in reference to English tradesmen, "prevail even in the higher grades of the commercial world. Innumerable frauds, untruth, both in words and in the principles of business, and carefully devised subterfuges are generally in vogue, while many of these have become established as commercial usages."[1]

In view of the universality of moral laxity in the commercial world, the alleged cause of success of the Jews in trade cannot be regarded as sufficiently well founded. In our opinion the success is mainly due to the personal qualities, historical conditions and present social position of the Jews. The sobriety, frugality and wonderful energy of the Jews, qualities which specially characterise them, are well known to all. Owing to their economy and thriftiness, the incidental charges on the purchase of goods are reduced, while the simple personal requirements of the Jew trader enable him to be satisfied with small profits on his goods, as also to sell them in the market at comparatively lower prices. Lastly the law, by closing to the Jews many branches of economic and social industry, and by crowding them together within a confined space of territory, makes them band themselves closely together and pursue their favourite occupation of trade. All these causes

---

[1] Herbert Spencer, Theoretical and Philosophical Essays, Vol. II., Article, "Commercial Morality."

added to the experience gained by them in trade, extending over a thousand years, reveal the secret of success of the superiority of the Jew traders over their Russian rivals, who not possessing the above qualities, and existing under totally different conditions of life, have to surrender the palm to the Jews in matters of trade. Mr. Aksakoff very justly observes in his " Investigation of Trade at the Ukraine Fairs," " that while a rouble will be turned over twice by a Russian trader, in the hands of a Jew it will be turned over five times."[1] A Jew merchant will consider himself lucky if he be able to sell his goods at a profit of two or three copecks per rouble, and it frequently occurs that he will sell without profit in order to realize his money the sooner and to employ it in another venture ; by rapidly turning over his available capital he reckons on increasing his gains in which he easily succeeds, thanks to the rapidity and convenience now existing for locomotion and communication. The Russian merchant on the other hand, is less active in the conduct of his business, a profit of two or three copecks on the rouble is beneath his notice, and he awaits a rise in price when he can at once secure a gain of 20 or 30 per cent. In consequence of such a difference in the mode of trading, the Jews become very dangerous rivals of the Russians in everything relating to business ; it is clear, however, that such rivalry is both desirable and

[1] Aksakoff, J. Investigation of the Trade at the Ukraine Fairs," St. Petersburg, 1858, page 36.

useful in the interests of the consumers. From the foregoing it would appear that the domination of the Jewish element in the commercial activity of the Western region is a completely natural phenomenon, and one that is inevitable under the present conditions of Jewish life. But it would seem from the complaints now heard of the Jews having secured to themselves all the trade in the Western region that here again they are guilty of some offence. When the Jews were allowed to educate their children in the common schools, and they did not at first willingly avail themselves of this right, they were accused of inveterate fanaticism and voluntary isolation. So soon, however, as the Jews began to send their children to the middle and higher schools, complaints were raised that these schools were being inundated by Jews. A numerical proportion for the admission of Jews into some institutions, and of Jew surgeons into the army was then at once established. And so with respect to the Jews it is in everything.

All such complaints and apprehension respecting the preponderance of the Jews in this or that sphere of public and economic activity would be perfectly natural and comprehensible if they were directed against an alien race having no organic connection with the Russian Empire. But the Jews have for many centuries been settled on Russian territory (in Poland and Lithuania) and for more than a hundred years they have been Russian subjects, paying taxes to the State and satisfying its exactions as the other subjects of the realm, though treated as regards their civil *status* only as half-citizens, deprived of common rights and equal protection of the law.

Such an abnormal and so humiliating a position of the Russian Jew subjects cannot but unfavourably affect the attitude of all Russians towards them. The latter are accustomed to regard the Jews as in a manner ostracized and as belonging, in the opinion of the legislature, to a pernicious class of individuals possessing, therefore, no interests in common with the bulk of the population. This accordingly gives rise to the widening of the breach between the Jews and the other inhabitants of the Empire, and it is to this state of things that the recent lamentable events in the South Western region in a great measure owe their origin. Putting aside, therefore, all considerations of justice, which exclude every ground for restricting the Jews in the right of freely electing their place of residence and preventing them pursuing any occupation that may not be forbidden by the general laws of the Empire, we consider that repressive measures in this respect cannot be recognised as satisfactory, and that it is necessary for the true interests of the State and as a matter of wise policy they should be abandoned.

All the foregoing leads us to the following general conclusions :—

1. Inasmuch as this system of preying on popular labour is a general phenomenon in the present

economic structure of national life, and seeing that its causes are to be traced to the very bases of the condition of the labouring classes, the measures necessary for struggling successfully with this evil should be mainly directed to the root of the evil, a detailed examination of which would be inappropriate on the present occasion.

2. For the re-establishment of more healthy relations between the Jews and the other inhabitants, and counteracting Jewish industrial and other exploitation in the Western region, it is necessary to grant the Jews complete civil equality and freedom of choice of residence. This would lead to a greater dissemination of the Jewish population, which is now crowded together in particular districts; to the alleviation of the poverty and hopeless condition of the Jewish masses, and would relieve the part of the country they now occupy from excessive industrial and other competition.

3. In order to destroy Jewish exclusiveness and to facilitate the fusion of the Jews with the rest of the population, it is necessary to incorporate the Jews with the local rural and urban communities, and to subject them completely in fiscal, administrative and other respects to the rules and regulations established for these communities. Those Jews who would wish to settle in the interior provinces should be allowed to enjoy the right of joining peasant and burgher

communities in the places of their new domicile, in the ordinary way.

4. It is at the same time necessary that serious attention should be directed towards the organisation of elementary schools for the juvenile Jewish population, inasmuch as the school must always be one of the principal instruments for the moral training and russification of the Jewish masses.

# APPENDICES.

## TABLE A.

RELATION OF INHABITANTS OF TOWNS TO THOSE OF VILLAGES OF PROVINCES WHERE JEWS ARE NOT ALLOWED TO RESIDE.

| Nos. | Names of Provinces and Provinces. | Town Population. | Rural Population. | Number of Inhabitants of Towns per 1000 of Rural Population. |
|---|---|---|---|---|
| 1 | Region of Don Cossacks | — | 317,120 | — |
| 2 | Viatka | 40,409 | 2,245,270 | 18·0 |
| 3 | Ufa | 28,859 | 1,268,603 | 22·7 |
| 4 | Vologda | 26,629 | 916,655 | 29·0 |
| 5 | Perm | 64,476 | 2,025,884 | 31·3 |
| 6 | Nijni-Novgorod | 41,848 | 1,132,278 | 36·6 |
| 7 | Voronej | 75,196 | 1,933,659 | 38·9 |
| 8 | Olonetsk | 11,282 | 264,406 | 42·7 |
| 9 | Riazan | 58,605 | 1,313,836 | 44·6 |
| 10 | Simbirsk | 50,650 | 1,080,827 | 46·9 |
| 11 | Penza | 51,791 | 1,052,653 | 49·2 |
| 12 | Kazan | 75,832 | 1,539,642 | 49·3 |
| 13 | Pskov | 34,481 | 684,778 | 50·3 |
| 14 | Kostroma | 54,300 | 1,022,202 | 53·1 |
| 15 | Kursk | 95,959 | 1,726,956 | 55·6 |
| 16 | Kharkoff | 83,590 | 1,483,934 | 56·3 |
| 17 | Samara | 97,995 | 1,641,290 | 59·9 |
| 18 | Esthonia | 17,455 | 287,487 | 60·9 |
| 19 | Orenburg | 35,456 | 569,964 | 62·2 |
| 20 | Tamboff | 118,511 | 1,898,563 | 62·7 |
| 21 | Archangel | 14,728 | 221,996 | 66·3 |
| 22 | Novgorod | 60,161 | 871,093 | 69·1 |
| 23 | Vladimir | 78,025 | 1,090,225 | 71·6 |
| 24 | Smolensk | 71,001 | 983,554 | 72·2 |
| 25 | Tver | 99,304 | 1,323,361 | 75·0 |
| 26 | Astrakhan | 43,305 | 508,869 | 83·1 |
| 27 | Tula | 95,472 | 980,142 | 97·4 |
| 28 | Yaroslav | 88,219 | 839,179 | 107·1 |
| 29 | Orel | 141,179 | 1,317,300 | 107·2 |
| 30 | Kaluga | 94,706 | 830,110 | 114·1 |
| 31 | Livonia | 97,737 | 848,417 | 115·2 |
| 32 | Saratoff | 182,334 | 1,458,146 | 124·4 |
| | Total | 2,129,495 | 35,748,030 | 59·6 Average. |
| 33 | Moscow | 253,693 | 1,371,189 | 185·0 |
| 34 | St. Petersburg | 205,933 | 701,761 | 293·5 |
| | Total | 459,626 | 2,072,950 | 221·2 |

# TABLE B.

Relation of Town to Rural Population in Provinces where Jews are allowed to reside.*

| Nos. | Names of Provinces and Regions. | Town Population. | Rural Population. | Number of Inhabitants of Towns per 1000 of Rural Population. |
|---|---|---|---|---|
| 1 | Poltava | 106,372 | 1,833,602 | 58·0 |
| 2 | Radom | 52,380 | 461,293 | 113·6 |
| 3 | Ekaterinoslav | 146,022 | 1,107,398 | 131·9 |
| 4 | Tchernigov | 183,091 | 1,337,138 | 136·2 |
| 5 | Courland | 80,325 | 508,066 | 158·1 |
| 6 | Kelets | 74,263 | 440,636 | 168·5 |
| 7 | Taurida | 98,010 | 546,345 | 181·2 |
| 8 | Suvalki | 80,908 | 425,492 | 190·2 |
| 9 | Kalish | 86,071 | 443,602 | 194·0 |
| 10 | Lomja | 76,949 | 394,571 | 195·0 |
| 11 | Plotsk | 73,754 | 362,347 | 203·5 |
| 12 | Vitebsk | 139,582 | 676,260 | 206·4 |
| 13 | Sedliets | 76,499 | 352,526 | 210·7 |
| 14 | Podolsk | 322,758 | 1,471,325 | 219·3 |
| 15 | Volhynia | 281,125 | 1,266,838 | 222·0 |
| 16 | Moghileff | 162,697 | 720,556 | 225·0 |
| 17 | Kieff | 392,731 | 1,600,450 | 245·4 |
| 18 | Minsk | 212,554 | 849,407 | 250·2 |
| 19 | Grodno | 189,209 | 743,209 | 254·6 |
| 20 | Wilna | 191,741 | 731,578 | 262·9 |
| 21 | Petrokoff | 136,201 | 492,769 | 276·4 |
| 22 | Kovno | 259,645 | 785,560 | 315·2 |
| 23 | Liublin | 163,115 | 571,222 | 319·0 |
| 24 | Warsaw | 203,683 | 610,409 | 337·0 |
| 25 | Bessarabia | 255,651 | 758,601 | 337·0 |
| 26 | Kherson | 479,867 | 943,846 | 500·8 |
| | Total | 4,525,210 | 20,304,397 | 222·9 Aver. age. |

* Both Tables are drawn up according to "Statistical Register," Table II. A.

The Tables A and B show that the average relation of the town to the rural population in 32 provinces, where the Jews are not allowed to reside, is as 59·6 per 1000, and in 26 provinces in which the Jews are domiciled, the average relation is 222·0 per 1000, in the two provinces containing the two populous capitals it is 221·2 per 1000, *i.e.* the average relation of the town to the rural population where the Jews are allowed to reside not only exceeds such relation in the provinces to which most of the Jews have no legal access by almost four times, but is even somewhat higher than the average relation of the town to the rural population in the provinces comprising the two capitals.

DARLING AND SON,

MINERVA STEAM PRINTING OFFICE,

35, EASTCHEAP, E.C.

www.ingramcontent.com/pod-product-compliance
Lightning Source LLC
Chambersburg PA
CBHW020123170426
43199CB00009B/611